How To Advertise:
A Handbook For
Small Business

by
Sandra Linville Dean

ISBN: 0-913864-38-2

Library of Congress Catalog Card No. 79-54981

Published by: Enterprise Publishing, Inc.
725 Market Street
Wilmington, Delaware 19801

For Lou Dean,
Katy Robbins, and my parents.

Table of Contents

Chapter 3: Public Relations And You

Chapter 4: Planning Your Ad Budget

Chapter 5: The Art Of Newspaper Advertising

Chapter 6: Radio In General

Chapter 7: The Radio Commercial

Chapter 8: Television In General

Chapter 9: The Television Commercial

Chapter 10: Magazines, Billboards, Bus Cards, Direct Mail

Chapter 11: Co-Op, Trade-Out, And Miscellaneous

Chapter 12: Planning Your Ad Campaign

Appendix: How To Select An Advertising Agency

Foreword

I once heard a television executive describe advertising in terms of a professional tennis match. He said most people who watch the top seeded players conclude that the game is really quite simple because the players always (or nearly always) play flawlessly. The ball goes where the player wants it, and rarely are there any goofs. But when the spectator steps out on the court to display the same graceful movements and skill, then it is all too apparent that there is much more to the game than it seems.

Advertising, he said, was the same way. Looking at the products produced by the top advertising agencies in the country makes it appear to be simple. Get the right photograph, write a few appropriate words, and bingo! You have an award-winning ad. All too often, the amateur advertiser finds out that advertising which does the job is not easy to produce.

This handbook will do the same for the amateur advertiser that Bill Tilden did for the weekend tennis player.

Stripped away is the murk which so often obscures advertising's only objective: to sell ideas, products, and public acceptance. The principles of advertising for the small business owner are exactly the same as those employed by the largest advertisers in the United States. Only the budgets differ.

HOW TO ADVERTISE nicely fills a publishing void which has existed too long. The modern entrepreneur who benefits from the easy-to-follow step-by-step discussions will be surprised to learn how simple, yet how complicated, this modern skill of advertising can be. More and more, small businesses are learning the principles which have sustained most of the corporate giants of this country. That is, first, produce a product or service for which there is a ready market and then inform that market in such a way as to create a desire for that product.

I have never seen a book on advertising which provides such a thorough and basic understanding of the dynamics of marketing. Happily, the goals set in the first chapter are met throughout the book. The mystery of advertising and communication through public relations is solved, and the complex elements are simplified.

Who, for example, would consider business cards and stationery to be part of the overall marketing scheme? And who goes behind the scenes at the print shop to *personally* insure there are no errors? These are but two early points which are often overlooked by those venturing into the world of advertising for the first time.

But if there is one service this book provides which eclipses all the others is it keeps the novice advertiser from wasting money. Advertising is expensive enough, and the paths of product marketing are pitted with potholes of waste. Every media salesperson, whether representing newspapers, radio, television, or other periodicals, can make the same promises: "Advertise with me, and your problems are solved." These shortcomings can be avoided by following the elimination procedures discussed on media selection.

For the small business owner who wishes to become an advertiser, there is no more fundamental text on the subject.

Lee Whitehead

(Editor's note: Mr. Whitehead is the Director of Public Relations for one of the fifty largest corporations in the U.S., and is accredited by the Public Relations Society of America. Formerly, he was a part of the marketing department, serving as Public Relations Director, for one of the world's largest hotel companies. He is also currently a member of the adjunct faculty of Arizona State University, teaching a course in Public Relations Techniques.)

Acknowledgements

Thanks for assistance, either tangible or intangible,
to Lou Dean, Mrs. W.H. Linville,
Robert H. Bowers Graphics, C.D. Ellis, Lewis Madison,
L.O. Long, Jr., Mrs. Gertrude Curtler.

Chapter 1
Why It Pays To Advertise

If you are in business, any business (whether it's selling lemonade at a roadside stand, or selling yourself as a special consultant, or running a retail store), somehow you must let your consumers know you are there. IT PAYS TO ADVERTISE.

True, but only if the advertising reaches those people to whom your product or service will be of interest. Advertising is a complex, but not mysterious, business. It is the means by which you communicate with your consumers.

The Simplest Route

The easiest way to advertise is to hire yourself a reputable advertising agency. A good agency will research your company, its problems and objectives and budget, and bring back a planned advertising campaign. It will handle all the technical aspects of creating the advertisements, place them according to plan, check to be sure they run correctly, review the billing from the media, and send you only one monthly bill. These services will cost you somewhere between 15% and 40% of your advertising budget—and sometimes more, if the agency thinks you can afford it. It is a good service, if the agency is good, and if your budget will stand it.

Maybe it won't. Maybe you are just starting out, and you have to generate some income before you have the money to advertise. (In order to generate that income, of course, you are going to have to advertise.) Or, maybe you have been in business for awhile, and have done some advertising, but it isn't bringing you the results you think it should.

Two Assumptions

For the purposes of our discussion, two assumptions have been made. First, you don't want to go the ad agency route, and second, that you (or possibly an assistant working closely with you) will be handling the advertising.

Based on these assumptions, there is one thing you need to know NOW. Advertising takes time; time to analyze your problems and goals, time to plan, to create ideas, time for research, time to produce ads, place them, monitor them, check the billing, and pay the bills. If your business can stand your spending money better than spending time, reconsider the ad agency. It might save you money, and will certainly save you time. (For those of you who wish to do this, either now or in the future, a guide is included in the Appendix to help you make a selection.)

In order to do your own advertising, and make effective use of your money, you will need to know what to do and how to do it. You will need to learn how to do what an ad agency would do for you, if you had one.

Don't let that idea frighten you. There is nothing really difficult about it, other than making sure you *take the time* to do it properly.

This book will give you the guidelines you need. Some segments may not apply to your business or budget, but for anyone who plans to advertise, there is a first step.

First Things First

Who are you?
What are you selling?
To whom are you selling it?

Before you learn to read, you must learn the alphabet. Before you can advertise effectively, *you* must know *what* you are selling *to whom*.

This is very important! During my years with an ad agency, I have found that this primary identification problem is always a big hurdle for new businesses to jump. It can also be difficult for some older businesses who haven't taken the trouble to get their acts together. Much of the time, a business will open, operate for six months to a year or longer, and then come to the agency screaming, "HELP! No one knows where we are! We have no traffic! What can we do?" etc.

More often than not, these businesses have no constant image. Perhaps they have a big sign out front, some stationery, they have run some newspaper ads, maybe they have been on the radio—and still they have no traffic.

The reasons for this are usually obvious. A sign painter has painted them a lovely sign (using Olde English lettering which no one can read); the stationery has the name, address, and phone number (printed in orange on red paper); the newspaper ad used the Olde English type (and listed every single item in the store); the radio spot listed all the items, had the name of the store buried in the middle, and gave no address at all. The miracle would have been if anyone at all had connected any of the advertising to the business.

I exaggerate, of course. But, I assure you, I've seen cases almost as bad. To help you see where you stand, answer the questions on the following checklist:

Figure 1. Questions to ask yourself about your business.

1. Does your business have a name? ____yes ____no
2. Is the name easy to remember? ____yes ____no
3. Is the name always printed in the same type style (script, gothic, and block letters are samples—see the illustration) on your letterhead, envelopes, billheads, checks, store front, newspaper ads? ____yes ____no
4. Do you have a logo? (A symbol which, when seen, *instantly* recalls your business. Shell and GE are examples.) ____yes ____no
5. If you have a logo, is it used wherever possible? ____yes ____no
6. Is your address clear and always consistent? ____yes ____no
7. Is your phone always answered politely, in a friendly voice, with the name of your business?____yes ____no

If all (or most) of your answers were affirmative, you are on the right track. Whether you were aware of it or not, you have begun establishing an image for your business. You have made progress in deciding who you are. The important thing is to be consistent. Always.

For example, if you are John Smith, a photographer, your business name might be:

Photography by Smith
-or-
John Smith Photography
-or-
Images by Smith

Your logo might be a camera beside the name.

Figure 2. Defining your image

Photography by SMITH ▮◼▮

In the above example, use of the familiar large camera immediately says "professional photographer," and the clean typestyle with emphasis on the name "Smith" would make this an easy logo to use in almost any advertising or printed matter. For example, it lends itself to use on letterhead, envelopes, a sign, business cards, direct mail pieces, gift certificates, and magazine and newspaper ads.

Here are some further examples of typestyles, to give you an idea of how type can be appropriate for use by a particular business.

Figure 3. Typestyles

THE STORE   Too ornate; illegible.

THE STORE   Ultra condensed, difficult to read.

THE STORE   Medium condensed, better.

The Store   Normal type face, initial capitals & lower case—alternative for condensed.

THE STORE   Good traditional type—suggests elegance.

THE STORE   Same type family as above—completely changes image.

THE STORE   Good, legible style.

The Store   Some scripts (not too fancy) suggest hand lettering.

The Store   Somewhat extreme, but works well, particularly in caps. & lower case.

As you can see, some styles are easier to read, some look inappropriate for the name of the business, and some look as though they might work.

To let you see specifically how the typestyle you choose can work *for* you or *against* you to create the image you desire for your business, let's look at three specific types of businesses: a hardware store, a bridal shop, and a lighting design and fixtures business.

Figure 4. Type inappropriate to the nature of the business.

Happy Hardware

Juliet Bridal Shop

ARIEL LIGHTING DESIGNS

The typestyle for the hardware store is not a bad style, but it is certainly a little fancy, and perhaps slightly effeminate for a hardware store. The type for the bridal shop, on the other hand, is too heavy, and gives no hint of the delicacy to be expected from such a feminine business. The type for the lighting store might have been chosen to create a "designer" feel, but is far too difficult to read to be a good type for a logo. In all three cases, though the styles by themselves are not "bad," they are definitely inappropriate. They do nothing to create an effective image for the business.

Figure 5. Effective type for logos.

Happy Hardware

Juliet Bridal Shop

ARIEL LIGHTING DESIGNS

The difference should be obvious. Here, the hardware store is using a bold, easy-to-read type that certainly has a more "masculine" feel than the type on the left page. The bridal shop has chosen a type that looks almost as personal as script, with a little flair that makes it feminine. The lighting store is using a simple type that conveys the feeling of "designer" which they were trying to reach before. In this case, however, the style is much easier to read, and will be far more appropriate for use in a wide range of advertising, from letterhead to newspaper ads.

As you can see, your choice of a typestyle to represent your business will affect how your customers see you; it will immediately convey an image to their minds, so be careful when you choose.

To take this subject one step further, let's discuss logo symbols for a moment. First, you need to be aware that you do not *have* to have a logo. If you already have one, fine. There is no need to go to the expense of having a new one designed. However, if you are still in the dark, and would like to know what such a symbol looks like and how it might be incorporated into your chosen name and typestyle, here are some examples:

Figure 6. Personalized logos.

Again, using the businesses we have just discussed, you can see how a logo can become a part of the name of the business. The hardware shop has chosen to use a hammer, which is certainly appropriate. The hammer is incorporated directly in the name. The bridal shop symbol, when used with this simple but effective typestyle, creates the correct image for that business. The lighting symbols point up the delicate type for the lighting store, giving it a little more emphasis than is achieved with the type alone.

Whether you already have a logo, or want to have one designed, keep in mind that it should convey the exact image you desire. Once you have selected it, use it on all printed matter—everywhere!

Every printed piece coming out of your place of business should carry this same logo and name, and the name should always be in the same typestyle. The phone should be answered, "Photography by Smith," *not* "Hello?" or "Good morning, may I help you?"

If you don't know who you are, how can you tell someone else?

Before you go any further, be *sure* this is what you want your name and logo to be (if you are already in business). It is horrendously more expensive to change a name or an image after it has become identifiable than it is to establish it in the first place.

If you are sure of who you are, the next thing to do is to decide *what* you are selling, and *to whom* you are selling it. For example, as the owner of a retail carpet store, you can choose to sell:

- Brand names
- Discount prices
- Super service
- The **largest** selection in town
- The **finest** quality in town
- The **easiest** terms in town
- The **best** location in town

or a combination of several of these (brand names at a discount, or the finest quality at the easiest terms). Before you decide, take a look at your possible customers. Decide whether you want to sell primarily to young marrieds, blue collar workers, rich people, or the whole town. Look at the population of your city. Is it mostly industrial workers, financial planners, farmers, or a combination? As a matter of efficiency, your advertising dollars would be allocated in different ways for different audiences and potential customers.

On the other hand, you may be selling primarily a service (as in real estate). In that case, you still need a place to hang your hat. Are you planning to be:

- The most *reliable*
- The *friendliest*
- The *fastest*

- The *biggest*
- The *most personalized*

or a combination of several of these?

You must decide *what* you are selling, and *to whom* you are selling it before you start advertising. This is because advertising works best when it is directed toward those people who: (a) might be interested in your product or service, and (b) can afford it. The advertising for an automobile dealer who sells only $16,000 cars would differ in many ways from that of the carpet dealer selling discounted remnants.

Once you have decided who you are, what you are selling, and to whom you are selling it, you will be able to use practical suggestions on how to advertise. No suggestion is practical without this preliminary work on your part. Whether you are just opening a business, or trying to find some solutions to advertising problems, spend some time and thought and research on this primary identification of your business and customers.

If you are already in business, look at your customers. See whether most of them are under eighteen years of age, 18 to 24, 25 to 34, 35 to 49, or 49+ years of age. They may not *all* fall into one age group, but a trend should be obvious. If they are eighteen to 100 years old, you need to know that, too. Do they pay cash, use store credit, or charge cards? Are they primarily male, female, factory workers, or bank presidents? Try to find out what prompted them to come in or use your services. Was it advertising you have done, something a neighbor told them, or simply impulse?

Observing your customers for about two weeks to a month, during average business periods, will be invaluable. Make sure all of your workers understand how valuable their cooperation will be to you (and to them, eventually), and ask them to take a survey. Set up a simple form with those facts included which are valuable for you to know. Fill out as many as you can. Use walk-ins or last month's contracts. Any source is all right.

Figure 7. Sample customer profile form.

Age: 18-24___ 25-35 ___ 35-49 ___ 49+___
Approximate Family Income: Under $20,000___ $20-30,000___ $30-45,000___
Sex: Male___ Female___
Occupation: Homemaker___ White Collar___ Blue Collar___
Reason For Coming In: Advertising___ Radio___ TV___ Newspaper___ Recommendation___ Other___ Chance___
How Was Purchase Made?: Cash___ Credit Card___ Store Credit___

This is a sample form. Yours should be applicable to your own business. Each of your salespeople should fill out one of these on every customer he/she talks with. If cooperation is good, five or six check marks will give you a customer profile which will be an invaluable aid in planning your advertising. To make your own, type a full page (perhaps three per page) of forms, with lines as shown. Make copies, and cut to make single forms.

Make a tally of all the facts. You should be able to come up with a "customer profile" which tells you, for instance, that your primary customer is female, age 25-34, making $20,000 a year.

If you are just starting in business, or as additional research, check with your wholesalers, or a local newspaper, radio, or television station. Their media research departments have figures available from national surveys for many products and businesses. Normally, they are glad to share them with potential media buyers. Try to obtain facts from as many different media as is practical, since in some cases, such surveys are slanted to present (for instance) newspaper advertising in as favorable a light as possible. Ask for a "customer profile" for your business or service. You should be able to find one or more, though you may also receive a lot of information about how many hours per day that person spends reading the newspaper or listening to radio. Hold all of this, since it will be discussed later. It is one of the tools you will need to learn to use for effective advertising.

Be as thorough as you can in this initial phase. Every dollar you spend on advertising is wasted unless it helps you communicate with your potential customer—and you certainly can't communicate with your customers if you don't know who they are.

Chapter 2
The Next Step

Stationery

Once you have decided who you are, what you are selling, and to whom you are selling it, you can begin establishing your business image. One of the first steps most businesses take is to have letterheads, business cards, envelopes, and other stationery printed.

Many people don't realize that everything printed which leaves the business should have a visual relationship to everything else. For instance, if you write a letter to a potential customer, and drop in his office later to leave your card, the card should match the letterhead. It helps to ring a little bell in your customers' heads, letting them know they've heard from you before. On the other hand, if they liked what you had to say in your letter, but your card doesn't match it, it may take them quite awhile to realize the two belong to the same business.

If you already have letterheads, business cards, billheads, and so forth, stop and take a close look at them. Do they project a consistent image of your business or service the way you want the public to see you? If not, now is the time to change them, since any printed material (including newspaper or magazine ads) should make use of your logo, name, and type style presented on the letterhead and business cards.

There are specific points you should check to be sure your stationery is accomplishing your aims. If you already have them, this list will help you decide if your letterhead and business cards are true representatives of your business:

1. Is the name of your business easily readable on all your stationery and signs? (Try to look at it as though you'd never seen it before. Some type styles are so difficult to read, words make no sense at first glance.)

2. Are the address and phone number legible? (They should be the same on all printed matter, and the phone number should include the area code.)

3. Does the quality of paper used reflect the things you'd like people to think about your business?

4. If you have chosen colored paper stock and ink, do the colors reflect the image of your business, or are they based solely on personal preference?

   (Be objective. Personally, my favorite color is orange, but I don't necessarily think it's a good color for a letterhead!)

5. Most people seem to prefer standard sizes (8½″ × 11″ for paper and 3″ × 2½″ for business cards) since they fit neatly into files. What size are yours? (Certainly you may use a folded business card, but its folded size should be standard.)

   The following are a few examples of effective and ineffective letterheads.

Figure 8.

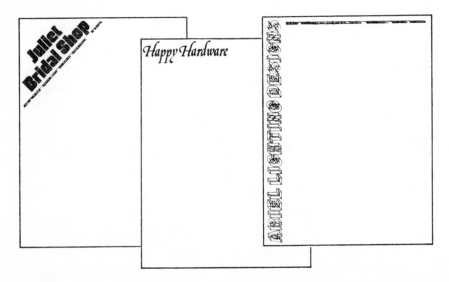

In Figure 8 are some samples of poor letterheads for your consideration. Note the fact that angles and typestyles make them difficult to read. The hardware store sample offers no address or phone number. The other two add nothing to the images of the business. At first glance, you may not be able to see the "design" elements, such as placement of logos on the page, which make these letterheads poor. Now glance at the illustrations below in Figure 9.

Figure 9.

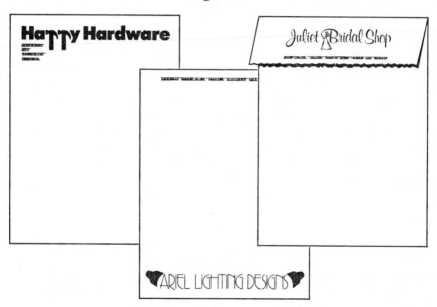

Can you see the difference? Not only are the typestyles more effective, but placement of the name and address are better in all three cases. The bridal shop has created an even more feminine look through the use of a simple fold in the paper. From these examples, you can begin to see why you may need help from an artist to design your new letterhead. Be sure you can look at these and see the difference, then go back and check your own letterhead/stationery again.

If you are not as happy as you were with your letterhead, or if you have not yet bought your stationery, here's how to do it:

Select your name, and decide what image you want your letterhead to project. *Exciting, fun, dignified, reliable* and *refined* are all words that describe intangible impressions you may wish to project. Have a firm idea in mind as to how you want your customers to see you.

Find an artist. You will need a commercial artist, who can produce the "mechanical art" necessary for a printer. Check the Yellow Pages of your phone directory, usually under "Artists—Commercial" or "Advertising Art." Call several of them, explaining that you need help with a letterhead and business cards, and ask to see samples of their work. The samples should be both creative and mechanically proficient.

When you see it, the work should be clean, neat, and obviously professional. It is normally mounted on art board with a tissue covering for protection.

The next step is to ask each artist for an estimate of charges to design and execute the mechanicals for your letterhead, envelopes, business cards, and any other stationery you might need. (By the way, while the artist is there, don't overlook your sign, if you have one. If the artist is doing artwork for everything else, he/she can produce the mechanical art for a sign painter.)

If you want the artists to design a logo symbol, their design charges may be more. If you want only your name, address, and phone number in a distinctive type style, the design charges should be less. The artist will expect to bill you for time, as well as for type.

Be careful. Don't go for the lowest price unless you are sure the work is good. Try to pick a price you can live with, quoted by an artist with whom you feel some degree of rapport. Consider such things as: whether the appointment was kept on time (will lateness be extended to your design work?); whether or not he/she listens to what you're trying to say, and seems interested in helping you, even if your ideas are nebulous; whether you like the person and feel comfortable; whether the artist is frank about this initial quote being the best guess, and whether he/she is willing to give it to you in writing. Remember, you are paying for creative ability and training as well as for the actual mechanical art being produced. Don't shortchange yourself by trying to be *too* economical.

Once you feel secure, and have made your selection of which artist you want to deal with, listen to what the artist tells you. There are things you may think are really great looking, really "different." But the artist may know from experience and training that these graphics are not only difficult to read, but may be in bad taste as well. Once you have given your artist the go-ahead, set a date for him to return with ideas from which you can choose.

These ideas will be sketches, not finished artwork. Look at all of them as objectively as you can. When you think you have decided which one you prefer, picture that one blown up to billboard size, and reduced way down to the smallest you can imagine using it. It should remain clear and easy-to-read at any size. Try hanging all versions in a place where you will see them several times a day for two or three days. One should begin to stand out as your favorite.

As soon as you have chosen the design, you will confer with your artist on the type of paper to be used. The weight of the paper, the texture, and the color will all have a bearing on the way the finished products will advertise your business. Choose carefully.

Also at this time, you will choose the ink color(s) to be used. Your artist will probably have suggestions. For instance, a light beige or cream-colored paper stock may look quite attractive with a rich, dark brown ink, and at the same time create just the image you have in mind. Of course, black ink on good quality white stock is always acceptable, but is certainly not the most imaginative choice you can make.

Your artist will now produce the mechanical art needed for the printer. It is from these mechanicals that a printer will print your stationery. Therefore, I caution you to *BE ABSOLUTELY CERTAIN THAT EVERYTHING ON THE MECHANICALS IS CORRECT.* Check and double-check. Have at least one other person who knows your business well check to be sure that spelling and phone numbers and addresses and capital letters and punctuation are exactly right. The time to correct an error is now, not after 1,000 letterheads have been printed.

Choose a printer. It is not necessary that you know precisely how the printer does his job, but you should select a printer in the same way you selected your artist. Plan to visit three or four printers, taking all your mechanicals along. (Be very careful when handling them. They should be protected by tissue, and carried in an envelope.) Someone in each printing firm will be in charge of estimates, and it is to this person that you will show your art. It will be necessary to know how many of each item you will need, so decide on how many of each piece you will be likely to use in a six-month period, before you visit the printer. Ask for a quote on that number, and on increments of that number. For instance, suppose you think you will need 500 business cards. Ask for quotes on 500, 1000, 1500. 1500 letterheads, ask for quotes on 1500, 2000, 3000. 1000 envelopes, ask for quotes on 1000, 1500, 2000.

This is a good idea, because the printing price per piece decreases as the number printed increases.

The printer's quote will be based on the cost of the paper, the number of different colors of ink to be used, whether the piece is printed on both sides, folded, diecut, gold stamped, embossed, contains line art or half-tones. Each separate manipulation will cost something. A good printer will quote a price as low as possible, within reason, meaning a reasonable profit for the printing house! It is to your benefit to obtain several quotes.

While you are visiting printers, ask to see other samples of their work, checking to be sure it meets good standards. A good printed piece is unmistakably sharp looking. The photographs are clear, and the contrast is good (black is black, white is white, greys are clear); ink colors are pure, and the register is correct (solid colors butt against each other with no overlap or fuzzy edges).

Ask each printer to call you with a firm quote (and it is nice to get it in writing) within a specified time. Three days should allow time to check on paper stock and figure the price. If it takes much longer than that, delivery of your finished work might be likewise delayed. Once you have the quotes, consider carefully. Again, the lowest quote may not be the best, unless you liked and trusted the printer and the printer's work.

Choosing a fairly well-known, moderately-priced printer is usually a good bet. If the job is botched, the printer will probably make good. But don't forget, if the art work you gave the printer was incorrect, and a thousand pieces are printed, you will have to pay for it. A thousand incorrect letterheads is expensive scratch paper—and that's all it's good for.

A word of warning. Lots of people "know a printer" or know the "daughter of the man next door who paints really great pictures." Don't plan on using these people unless you go through the steps I've outlined, and find the person you "know" is the best choice. A professional will respect your professionalism. Letterheads printed in someone's basement are probably going to look as though they were printed in someone's basement.

Internal Attitudes and External Image

So, you're all set. The doors are open, the sign is up, the business cards are in your pocket, and the staff is ready and waiting.

Are they? Whether your staff is yourself and a part-time secretary, or ten salespeople plus delivery personnel, installers, mail clerks, and others, have you taken the time and trouble to explain to each one of them exactly what you expect, as well as what help they can plan on getting from you? Is each staff member completely aware of methods of operation, as well as knowledgeable about your product or service? All the advertising in the world can't help you if your customers are unhappy. And they will be unhappy if they contact someone who obviously doesn't know the answers to their questions, who does not appear to know the job, or who perhaps seems not to care about them.

I do not profess to know how to run your business. I do know from experience that an unhappy staff, or a confused staff, will cause unhappy customers. If you have spent advertising dollars to bring people to your business, you certainly do not want them turned off, or discouraged, or irritated by your staff.

Word of Mouth

Besides which, each person who leaves your place of business unhappy will probably tell two or three other people, and these potential customers will make a concerted effort to stay away. That brings us to a form of advertising which is sometimes overlooked. It is totally free of dollar cost. In fact, you can get this form of advertising whether you want it or not. It is called "word of mouth."

The only control you have over word-of-mouth advertising is your control over your business. Happy, satisfied customers, who are sure they have had fine treatment, who are pleased with your product, attitudes, and services, will spread the word for you.

So will unhappy customers.

The only thing to be recommended directly is "supercourtesy." Whatever your line of business, sit down and think of ways and means of assuring your customers of the finest service possible. How can you also assure them that you appreciate their business? For instance, one of the easiest things you can do is to send a follow-up thank you note. It should be carefully worded (even if you create a "form letter") to sound like an individual note. It should always be an original, typed on your letterhead, with at least a line or two referring to something within the transaction which proves the salesperson writing the note remembers the person. It should ask whether the customer is satisfied, and any complaints should be promptly and graciously attended to. You will undoubtedly be able to think of other ways to improve and protect your customer relationships, thereby assuring your word-of-mouth advertising is the best possible.

The Media

Use of the media is the accepted way for any business to communicate with its customers, both current and potential. Television, radio, newspaper, magazines, billboards, bus or taxi cards, direct mail, telephone directory listings are all media. Leaving out only the directory, these can be called "major media," due to the fact that they hit a large number of the population. There is another category, sometimes confusing to new advertisers, which can be called "miscellaneous."

Goodwill Advertising

Into this category falls "goodwill advertising," or advertising that is supportive to some part of the community. It includes ads placed in high school yearbooks, university sports programs, community events, and so forth. The ads usually cost a minimal amount, but unless it is carefully policed and distributed, expenditure in this category can far outweigh value. There are several ways to handle it:

A. **Refuse everyone.** Explain that since budget does not allow you to include everyone, you prefer not to cause hard feelings by choosing one over another.

B. **Budget.** Set aside a sum to be used for this purpose. When it is gone, explain that the budget for this year has been used, but you'll be happy to consider them for next year. Keep a list of what you bought, and the cost, and with it a list of those you turned down. The idea is to be fair in distributing money.

C. **Select.** Choose those schools, or community events, which you think might really be of value in building your business. For instance, a bridal shop would perhaps place ads in local high school yearbooks; a car dealer might invest in an ad in the local university basketball program, aimed at alumni who might buy cars.

The most important point to keep in mind is to control the amount of money spent. If you cannot afford these courtesy ads, do not buy them.

However, if your business is located in a small town, where major media are scarce or non-existent, ads of this type may be one of your primary advertising options. In that case, their use would obviously be an important part of your budget planning.

The major media listed at the beginning of the section can be divided into two broad categories: *broadcast* and *print*. Broadcast includes radio and television. Print is anything which must be read, and includes newspapers, magazines, direct mail, and such things as ads in telephone directories. Billboards and bus/taxi cards are also print, but are more properly called "outdoor" advertising.

There are differences in all the media. The differences make the use of each media more effective for some businesses than others, or more effective at different times of the year. Here is a brief description of each of the major media, to help orient you to their uses. We will discuss each one more completely in the following chapters.

Television

TV combines visual image with audio. It allows you to "show and tell" your potential customer exactly what service or product you offer. Due to the combination of images, TV is often considered the strongest advertising medium you can use. It can also be, or appear to be, the most expensive.

Radio

Radio relies on audio image to attract attention and create interest. It must be carefully created and placed, in order to give the best results. If this is done, a radio campaign can go a long way toward establishing your identity in the minds of customers. Radio is not usually as expensive to produce or to run as television advertising, and can be quite an effective medium for the small advertiser.

Newspaper

Until fairly recently, newspaper advertising was the major expenditure in almost every ad budget. However, as our society has become more mobile and faster-paced, as television news coverage has become more complete, and as spare time has become more valuable, newspaper readership has begun to drop. It is still an excellent medium, and can be used to great advantage by the small advertiser, as long as limitations are remembered, and careful planning and ad design are aimed at accomplishing specific goals.

Magazines
If your city has a local magazine or two, an ad placed here can be of benefit. Most local magazines will (from time to time) have special sections or features which might be closely connected in some way with your business or service. Careful monitoring of these features will show you where and when your ad should run.

Billboards/ Bus Cards
Outdoor advertising can be a valuable extra medium, either for establishing image, or as a directional aid. Since a person driving past a billboard has only a few seconds to read and grasp a message, this form of advertising must be carefully designed to be effective.

Direct Mail
Direct mail can be used very effectively by the small business if it is well-planned and professionally executed. It may be used as an announcement of a special sale or as an urgent appeal to your customer to act *NOW*, including an order form right in his hot little hand. Since mailing anything is expensive today, a direct mail campaign must be designed and planned to bring you specific results, in order to be an efficient advertising medium.

These are the major advertising media. There are other major forms of advertising, each of which you must consider on its own merits as directly related to your business or service. A partial list of these forms includes:

Local Business Directories – can be put out by the Chamber of Commerce, inserted in a local magazine, or published by an enterprising person who sells a group of businesses the ads.

Bowling Alleys/Sports Arenas – ads sold on score sheets, programs, or walls.

Theatre Programs – live theatre.

Special Event Programs – a tennis tournament, or Little League championship.

Newcomer's Guides — The Chamber of Commerce can have a hand in this, or the local magazines.

Welcome Wagon Gift Certificates.

Calendars.

Specialty Advertising

Also included in this area is Specialty Advertising, which means all those free gifts with your name on them: pens, pencils, pocket calendars, key rings, litter bags, rain scarves, etc.

Giveaways such as these are a large temptation to the small advertiser. Anything with your name on it can seem like a great idea. After all, as the salespeople will be sure to point out, it will cost you only a few cents per item. Sure. And 5,000 pens at 5¢ each is $250.00 out of your ad budget.

If a person is in your store looking over your merchandise, a pen is not going to make him buy. If he's not in your store, a pen is not going to make him come in. But a $250.00 newspaper ad, or radio schedule, could bring you several customers. If you feel you absolutely *must* give something away, make it useful—perhaps an item directly related to your business or service. This might include a free doormat to a carpet customer; a key case to the proud owner of a new car; a frame for a portrait; a protective folder for a new insurance policy. But, be *sure* the money you spend this way is worth more to your advertising goals than the newspaper ad or radio schedule. It is almost impossible to put any sort of effective advertising message on an item of this type. As a result, much of the time a free gift is merely a token of thanks to your customers. If you can afford it, fine. If not, don't do it. Say thank you, instead. It won't cost you a thing, and can be just as effective.

Public Relations

Another form of advertising, not so easy to pin down, but much discussed by larger companies and their ad agencies, comes under the broad heading "public relations." In a large corporation, this field can be quite involved, including all sorts of things from news releases about a speech the company president made, to announcements of new products, to the opening of new plants. Sometimes this involves huge parties for the media and interested businesses.

It is an extremely complex field, and a skillful "PR person" can draw an enormous salary based on his/her value to the company. If you are interested in how public relations really works, do some reading. Your library will have books, ranging from textbooks for PR classes, to books of stunts which have worked for other people. Most bookstores carry a selection. For our own purposes, a brief discussion of public relations in a small way will be included in the next chapter, with some ideas which may be of use to you as a small business or service.

Chapter 3
Public Relations And You

Media Reps

Whether you have already opened your business, or are about to do so, the word will get around to the various media in your area. You will immediately be besieged by their salespeople. These charming people tend to appear to me like a flock of particularly enterprising, well-dressed buzzards, each of whom is grabbing as big a piece of the action as possible.

The fact you must absolutely always keep in mind is that you are paying their salaries. They are paid on commission. Some percentage of your advertising dollar winds up in the media rep's pocket. This is the reason they are so enterprising and enthusiastic. In fact, many of them are downright pushy. Each of them will show up in your office with "absolute proof" that his/her radio station, or magazine, or newspaper, or billboard campaign, is the *one* form of advertising you need to "put you on the map."

Nonsense.

No *one* form of advertising is perfect. No *one* radio station, or other medium, will be able to bring your message to the attention of every one of your prospective customers.

Until you are ready to buy some media, send them away. Ask them to (a) leave a card, so that you may contact them personally when you are ready to buy, and (b) to send you the latest survey figures on their audiences, as well as a thirteen-week proposal on how much advertising they believe you need using their particular medium. Ask them to include the following information:

Figure 10. Information to ask of media reps.

Name: *theirs and the medium they represent.*
Address:
Phone:

Audience information: *(who they reach; ages, incomes, best times of day, areas of the city)*

A current rate card

An efficient 13-week schedule, showing:
> Cost per ad
> Cost per week
> Cost per month
> Cost for the schedule
> Specific placement of each ad they recommend, day by day

A paragraph summary of how and why they believe this schedule will benefit your business.

This will accomplish a couple of things. It will get them out of your hair for a bit, until you know more about what you are doing. It will give you the beginnings of a file on the available media in your area, and it will begin to give you a feel for how reliable and helpful each of them will be.

The easiest way to do this is to type up a sheet listing the information you need. Make a bunch of copies and pass one out to each media rep who calls on you. It is not a bad idea either to give them a few facts to work with. Go back to that survey you did on your current or probable customers, and give them a brief summary. It might go something like this: "Our primary target is the working woman, age 25 to 35, with an income of at least $20,000. The secondary target is the 18 to 24 year old woman either working or attending college." Type the whole thing on your letterhead.

There is no reason at this point to give them an accurate budget figure, though they will probably ask. You might give them an arbitrary (it should be within the realm of possibility) figure for your total ad budget for thirteen weeks. Some of them will use up the entire budget on their medium alone. Others will realize you will probably need other media as well, and use a portion. A good media rep will be sensible and will base recommendations on an efficient use of the medium. He/she will try to help you, not merely sell you.

You should be aware that media reps can absorb an enormous amount of your time, if you are not careful. Be stingy with it. Be firm. You cannot buy advertising from all of them, so some will have to be disappointed. However, at this stage, you should assure them that their cooperation is much appreciated, and that they will be considered in your planning.

Reps to watch out for

Above all, do not let yourself be snowed by the slap-on-the-back, hail-fellow-well-met glad-hander who comes on as your latest and greatest friend. This guy will wine and dine you and stroke your ego, and with big words and bigger promises offer you the best deal and the lowest prices in town. He/she will wheel and deal and tell you you're getting a lower price than your competitor.

A reputable media rep, working for a reputable company, will sell off the published rate card. Ethical reps will help you schedule your ads and spots to the best advantage, and if a "package" is available to you, it will be available to everyone. They will prove their statements with facts and figures. They will present you with options and explain their differences. They will be business people themselves, so they won't take up any more of your time than is necessary. They will come across as sincere and honest, and if they say they will do something, it will get done, and done on time. They may occasionally offer to take you to lunch, but they are quite likely to talk a little business while you are eating.

A good rep will check in with you once or twice a month, but won't harrass you every two or three days. If you have nothing for your media rep, he/she won't whine that they sure need the business, they will merely make a polite request that you let them know if you need them. They will keep you posted on rate changes—the ones that save you money as well as the raises. A good media rep treats you with the same courtesy and professionalism you show your customers. They can be invaluable.

Public Relations

While you are going through the planning of your paid advertising, you can make use of whatever public relations (or free advertising) you can dig up in your area. Here are a few ideas:

1. **A news story** about the opening of your new business, or a new service you will be providing, sent to your newspaper. A news release should be typed, double-spaced, on your letterhead. Read your paper(s) very carefully for a full week to discover where such an article might be acceptable. Would it be business page? Financial page? "Home" page? Call to find out the name of the person in

charge of that page. Call or send a brief letter, explaining that you are sending a release. An example of a news release:

Figure 11. News release—new store announcement.

FOR IMMEDIATE RELEASE

    Mr. John Jones announced today the January 23 opening of a new woman's clothing store at 622 South Elm Street. To be called THE STORE, the new business will offer a full line of clothing for the working woman. A special consultation service will be provided to assist each customer with making the correct choices to suit her own personality and tastes, in conjunction with the appropriate dress for many specific businesses, such as banking, selling, general office work, and others.

    The special consultant, Ms. B. B. Smith, has previously performed this service for the Department Store in Houston, Texas. She is a graduate of Smith University, with degrees in both Fashion Design, and Business Management.

Send a picture of Ms. Smith, or a picture of the store front. It should be at least 5″ × 7″ (8″ × 10″ is usual), black and white, glossy. Print your store name and address on the back, and paper clip it to the article. A photograph can be a big help in making your article appear more interesting.

Figure 12. News Release—new service business announcement.

FOR IMMEDIATE RELEASE

TO: Local Media

FROM: J. J. Thomas

RE: New Service

Mr. J. J. Thomas, formerly with Briar, Wood and Williams,
Accountants, announced today the opening of a new, personalized
bookkeeping service for self-employed persons. Your Personal
Accountant, to be located at 1 South Main Street, will handle
all phases of bookkeeping, taxes, and other financial records
for the one-man business.

Another form of news release makes use of a special event.

Figure 13. News Release—seminar announcement.

FOR IMMEDIATE RELEASE

TO: Local Media

FROM: Mr. James Thomas

        President/Fancy Cameras, Inc.

RE: Special Seminar

Mr. James Thomas, President of Fancy Cameras, announced today
that Allen Arrow, world famous wild-life photographer, will
hold a seminar on "Photographing Pets" Wednesday, July 18,
at the City Auditorium. The seminar is open to the public
at no charge, but reservations must be made in advance, as
seating is limited. Call Fancy Cameras for further information.

2. **A radio or television talk show visit.** Usually, this must involve something you do that is of interest to a *lot* of people. For example, if you are a carpet retailer, you might discuss what the consumer can expect from new fabrics, or what to expect from good installation of wall-to-wall carpet. A plumber might talk about the kinds of pipes available, and why they are good and bad, and what to expect from a reputable plumber. The idea is to take some facet of your business which presents a problem to or raises questions from consumers, and elaborate or explain. Check with your local stations for the availability of any such program, and get the name of the person running it. The thing to remember here is that they *will not* accept you unless the subject will be of interest to their audience. Which means most everyone.

3. **Speaking engagements** at local clubs or schools. This is no time to be shy. If you are, work on getting over it, at least to the point where you can handle a simple twenty-minute talk. Check your library or bookstore for books which tell how to organize such a talk, and how to inject a little humor. Once you're fairly secure, call the schools or clubs and offer your services. The talk should offer assistance or information related to your business or service. A bridal shop owner can talk to high school or college groups about "how to plan a wedding," to clubs for older women about what is expected from mothers of brides and grooms. Sit down and see how many groups might be interested in some aspect of your business, and work up your talk. Then call and offer it. If you do speak at a large, well-known club or school, send a brief release to your paper(s). Also, at this sort of meeting, you can hand out a sheet listing the topics you cover, and thus get your name and address and phone number into the hands of everyone attending.

4. **Hold a class** in your place of business. Send a brief announcement to all local radio stations and the newspaper. See the examples below for facts to include. The class should be free, or costs should be minimal, and it should be informative and of interest to a majority of your customers. Again, you can hand out an information sheet.

Figure 14. News Release—special class announcement.

```
TO:  Mr. John Jones         For Release:  Jan. 21 - 23
     Radio Station QQQQ
RE:  Decorating Class
     The Store, at 222 West Main Street, will offer a
free seminar on Home Decorating, Wednesday, January 23,
at 8 p.m.  The seminar is open to the public.
```

5. Check with your wholesalers or suppliers. They sometimes have **people available to give talks** of one sort or another. For instance, hardware stores generally sell a wide range of products, ranging from paint to tools to garden supplies. In such a case, someone might be available from a nationally-known tool company to give a demonstration of the latest uses of a particular saw. Or a garden product company might be in town to answer specific questions on use of their products, as well as general questions on lawn and garden care. Manufacturers representatives are sometimes available for answering questions on electronics equipment, such as stereos, car tape players/radios, or other kinds of equipment. Carpet manufacturers sometimes have people who can help with home decorating questions.

6. Even if your business does not at first glance appear to offer any opportunities such as these, you can probably find something if you dig. You'd think a tire dealer/automotive repair service might not have many ways to use public relations. But he can create a simple talk on the importance of always keeping a car in top running condition, for safety's sake as well as from the standpoint of economical operation. The talk can then be offered to high school driver education classes, as well as to various men's or women's clubs. He can offer a free check-up for the people attending, thus getting his name into the community eye.

Public relations is a way for you to become more personally recognized by those people who are customers or potential customers. If you are a new business, it is a particularly good way for you to begin establishing your reputation, as well as to gain some recognition. The suggestions offered here have worked; you may be able to come up with others equally as good, or better.

If you will take the time, you will probably be able to discover a number of such activities taking place in your city. There may be a column in the newspaper announcing such things, or a local radio station may have announcements from time to time. If your activity is free, or even if there is a nominal charge, and if it is open to the public, you can probably get the coverage you need to publicize it.

Before you go on, take a moment to re-read the examples of PR releases above. You will note that they are directed to a specific person, and that dates for their use are given. You will note that the subject is plainly stated, and that the actual message is brief and to-the-point. If typed on your letterhead, Mr. Jones will be able to call and ask further questions if he is interested or has a need to know something not included. It is very important that any release you send out should be as complete as possible.

Any public service or news release should include *who* is doing *what, when, where,* and *how.* It should be brief. It should be in the hands of the person who will run it approximately one week in advance of the date you would like for it to appear. Twenty-four to forty-eight hours ahead, call the person to whom it was sent. Ask if it was received, and express your appreciation for cooperation in running it.

By the way, if your business is open, hand all your customers a sheet explaining any class or talk you will be giving. Ask them to spread the word if it will be open to the public. If they are interested, they will come and bring a friend.

These are simpler ways to get your name out. You can do other wilder, things of course. The idea is to sit down and think of friendly, or exotic, or unusual means of letting people know who you are and where you are. Stay within the bounds of good taste, and spend as little money as possible.

A P.R. Person For You

If you can't think of anything to do, try looking around for an "idea" person. You may have someone within your own organization who can make suggestions. Or you may have a friend-who-has-a-friend who wouldn't mind helping.

You will have to look for a person who can help you. People are not going to stop you on the street and offer their services. You may have to pay a fee, and you will have to decide for yourself whether or not their suggestions will work for you.

In spite of all this, if you are not ready to buy media, or hire a full-time P.R. person of your own, such a person may be able to help you. Incidentally, your friendly media rep may know a "real" P.R. person who works for an ad agency or public relations firm in your city. As long as such professionals are not handling the public relations for one of your competitors, they may be willing to do a little "moonlighting" for you.

Check around. It's worth a try, and you may find someone great.

Chapter 4
Planning Your Ad Budget

The basic premise of advertising is: *spend money to make money.* The big question is: "How much money should you spend?"

There are a number of questions you will need to answer before you can decide on an advertising budget. They are important, and you should find the answers before you actually buy any advertising at all.

Your Advertising Goals

First, you must decide what goals you expect to achieve through your use of advertising. Do you want your advertising dollars to bring people in every single day of the year, as though you're having a sale to end all sales? Do you want your ads to build an image in the minds of your prospective customers that establishes your business as the only place in town that offers personalized service? Are you trying to place your name so squarely in the public eye that it is the one name which comes to mind when your field of business is being discussed?

Many people tend to relegate an advertising budget to a place somewhere below the budget of a secretary and slightly above the budget of the people who clean the office. In fact, it should be ranked first in importance. First, because unless you can attract customers, in sufficient numbers to maintain the business, no one else is likely to be paid anything for very long.

This is particularly a problem for new businesses. Although a great deal of financial planning normally goes into the efforts to form a new business, most of us seem to forget that unless the public knows about us, we will not succeed. If you are just opening a business, do sit down and talk with your financial advisors about advertising. Try to be sure your plans include a reasonable amount of money to establish your business firmly in the eyes of the public. To help you do this, here are some suggestions.

Your Advertising Budget

Certainly, the decisions on how much money you will spend will finally rest with you. However, to start off, try using a figure that is between seven and ten percent of your expected annual gross income. Ten percent is not unreasonable. Four to six percent is average. Some real estate firms use one percent of their gross sales as the advertising figure, but real estate sales are normally much larger than sales in any other type of business. So the one percent translates into a fairly good-sized cash figure.

If you are just starting out, try pumping that media rep you trust for figures on how much your competitors spend. The rep won't and shouldn't divulge actual figures, but will probably try to help you with an educated guess.

If your accountant blows a gasket at 10%, find out what is a reasonable figure. Compare that with the guess on your competitor's spending. You must decide how much money you will be able to spend on advertising before you can spend it efficiently. The key to make advertising work for you is planning it. Then follow the plan. Try not to let your advertising budget become an afterthought. It should be one of your most important considerations.

How to Plan Your Advertising Budget

It may be easier for you to plan your budget if you have some idea what the final product should be. Using the 10% figure as a guideline, let's assume your projected gross income for the year is $50,000, thus giving you an advertising budget of $5,000.

Before you allocate one penny of this money to any media, review your advertising goals. Be specific.

If you are just opening your doors for the first time, you may want to consider a "Grand Opening" celebration. It can be an effective tool in helping you establish the fact that you are ready to receive customers. However, it can also use up a lot of your money.

How Seasons Affect Your Advertising Plans

Is your business one that has very specific selling seasons which you can expect to be busier than others? A gift shop, for instance, may want to consider advertising just before major gift-giving occasions such as Valentine's Day, Mother's Day, Father's Day, and Christmas.

Non-seasonal Advertising

Perhaps your business is one that does not depend on any special selling season, but instead would do better with a steady advertising program every month. No matter what type of business you operate, however, you will need to decide on a budget figure. Then plan how that money will be used. It is this type of planning that will enable you to get the most out of every dollar you spend for advertising. It is also the one area of advertising that many people find is the biggest roadblock. An ad agency cannot function unless the client is willing to commit a certain amount of money for purposes of advertising planning. So advertising planned by an advertising agency always seems to work better. If you are willing to plan in the same way, your advertising will work better.

Following are two examples of advertising budgets. The first uses the gift shop example of a limited budget and specific selling seasons.

Figure 15. Small retail shop budget.

Total Budget: $5,000.00

Grand Opening: Two-Day Sale
    1. Newspaper ads:
    A. Medium-size ad, evening paper, day before
       opening 200.00
    B. Larger ad, morning paper 300.00
    2. Radio schedule:
    A. Two stations, spots to run 3PM the day before, to
       3PM opening day 500.00
Valentine's Day
    1. Newspaper ad 2 days ahead 200.00
    2. Radio spots—same day as newspaper 200.00

Easter
    1. Newspaper ad/children's gifts 200.00

Mother's Day
  1. Newspaper ad 3 days ahead 200.00
  2. Radio spots—same day as newspaper 200.00
Father's Day
  1. Newspaper ad 3 days ahead 200.00
  2. Radio spots—same day as newspaper 200.00
Christmas—Three Weeks
  1. Newspaper—one ad per week 600.00
  2. Radio—2 days per week, first two weeks 750.00
  3 days Christmas week 750.00

Production Charges:
  1. Layout and design of two basic newspaper ads (one
     $300 size, for Grand Opening, one $200 size to be
     reused with different headlines) 200.00
  2. Radio production—sound effects, talent, studio
     charges if needed 150.00
Slush Fund—Use Where Needed 50.00
  Total Advertising Expenditures **$5,000.00**

Before you go on to the next budget, take a moment to re-read the above. You will note that any pens, pencils, high school yearbook ads, or other free gifts which might be classified as advertising, must come out of the $50 Slush Fund. A budget plan of this type eliminates unnecessary spending, provided, of course, that you stick to the plan.

As a further example, let's take a look at a new real estate firm dealing primarily in large estates and commercial property. The firm was formed by a merger of two others, and has projected a gross income of $3,600,000 for the first year. Their first objective is to become known in the market by their new name. The second is to continue selling the types of properties mentioned. All of this will require two distinct kinds of advertising. Their budget for a year might look like this:

Figure 16. Large service business budget.

Total Budget: $36,000.00
Reserved for advertising of specific properties: *10,000.00*

First Month:
    Television time 6,000.00
    Radio time 2,000.00
    Television production 1,000.00
    Radio production 200.00
Second Month:
    Television time 2,000.00
    Radio time 1,000.00
    Newspaper space 2,000.00
Third Month:
    Radio time 1,000.00
    Newspaper space 1,500.00
Fourth Month:
    Radio time 1,000.00
    Newspaper space 1,000.00
Fifth Month:
    Brochure
    (design/printing/mailing) 1,000.00
    Radio time 1,000.00
Sixth Month:
    Radio time 700.00
Seventh Month:
    Off
Eighth Month:
    Off
Ninth Month:
    Radio time 700.00
Tenth Month:
    Radio time 700.00
    Newspaper space 600.00
Eleventh Month:
    Radio time 1,000.00
    Newspaper space 600.00
Twelfth Month:
    Radio time 700.00
Newspaper Ad Production 300.00
Total Annual Advertising Expenditure $36,000.00

For this type of plan, where a large sum of money from the total advertising budget is set aside for a specific purpose, in this case the advertising of specific properties, it is wise to remember that even during the months (six to nine, above) when the image-building campaign is slight, the specific purpose ads should be designed so they continue to place the proper name, logo, and general appearance of the company (image) before the public.

That is, if the above real estate firm has designed an image advertisement for the newspaper, using a distinctive logo, type style, and border, these same components should be used in the ads for properties.

**Figure 17. The ad on the left promotes
the company image. The one on the right uses the same
components, while selling a specific property.**

Now, take a moment to look back at the two budgets. Although your own budget may be smaller (or larger), your eventual goal is to be able to plan your advertising in just this way. In order to do so, you will need to know how much money you will have available for advertising purposes for a year.

If you are just opening your business, try to have enough money available to enable you to advertise sufficiently to let your potential customers know who and where you are. Nothing is more discouraging to a new venture than a total lack of business. Just opening the doors is not enough. You can't expect any customers to come in unless you let them know you exist.

It may be totally impossible for you to project your advertising budget for a full year. If this is the case, try to decide on at least a thirteen-week budget at a minimum. That way, you will avoid having to make snap decisions at the crucial beginning of your advertising program. If you can plan the first thirteen weeks, and eight weeks into that plan start projecting the second thirteen weeks, your advertising can be a "campaign." It won't look like a hit-or-miss toss-up bought on the basis of whatever loose change happens to be on hand when a persuasive media rep knocks on your door.

By the way, thirteen weeks is the normal buy made on radio, television, and in the newspapers. It is not an arbitrary selection of mine. Some stations or papers allow advertisers a discount of from 5% to 15% if a contract can be written for at least thirteen weeks.

Reaching the Media

It's nitty-gritty time. At this point, you need to begin some factual research into the media in your area. This is not a guesswork game, not a personality game. It is a search for cold facts which will give you a base of information from which to make intelligent media selections.

First, go back to your "customer profile." Decide exactly whom you are trying to reach. You *must* do this first, since if your audience is a very specific or limited one, some media will be far more effective than others.

If you are sure you know exactly whom you are trying to reach with your message, you are ready for the next step. It's a big one, and usually not too easy.

Forget everything you think
you know about who is reading the newspaper.

Forget your opinions
on which TV shows are the best.

Forget your favorite radio station.

Forget, throw away,
put out of your mind ANY personal opinion
you may have about ANY of the media in your area.

It doesn't matter if you love the morning man who wakes you up every day. It doesn't matter if you hate rock music.

You are not going to buy media on the basis of your personal likes and dislikes. TO DO SO IS A WASTE OF MONEY.

An advertising agency, to be effective, must spend your money only where the *facts* prove it will get your message across to your target audience. An advertising agency must be objective. So must you.

These facts are available. there are detailed surveys made by nationally-known firms which will provide you with specific information. The surveys will cover who is reading, watching, or listening to what. You next step is to familiarize yourself with the actual surveys available in your area. A list of well-known surveys includes:

- STARCH—newspaper
- ARB (ARBITRON)—Radio and television
- PULSE—Radio
- NIELSEN—television/radio in some markets

These are nationally-known, and they serve most parts of the country. One or all of them should be available in your area. Go back to the sheets you requested from the media reps. They should have indicated the source of the audience figures given. If they did not, ask where the figures came from. If you live in a metro area of any size, you will quite probably find that the source used was one of the above surveys.

Read all the sheets carefully. From them, you should begin to get an overview of where your audience is, as well as some idea of what sources are available for information.

A radio survey will include variations on the following types of information:

1. A designation of the geographical area being surveyed.
2. A figure indicating total population.
3. The call letters (and other information) on the stations included in the survey.

4. Specific figures showing how many people are listening to any station at any given times during the broadcast day. The people are normally divided by age and sex categories.

A television survey will indicate the population, the number of households owning television sets, specific program times and names, and the number of households, men, women, children, or adults estimated to be watching each specific program.

In order to place your advertising effectively, you must therefore know whether your primary target is male and/or female, and the approximate age grouping. If you sell tires, and the person who is most likely to buy them is a 25-year-old man, you do not want to buy ads during a program aimed specifically at 6-year-olds, or at women over the age of forty.

Once you have defined your audience, take some time to learn to read the actual surveys. To make it easy on yourself, try to find one media rep from each of the media in your area who is willing to help. Explain that you really do not understand the survey figures and ask for an hour's time. Be frank in saying that you would like to look at the actual survey and have them explain it to you.

It may cost you four or five hours total time, but once you know what the audience figures are telling you about each station or newspaper or magazine, you can choose where and when to place your advertising. Even if you have no choice of stations (unlikely in most cities), you will have a choice of days and hours. Some of these will obviously be more beneficial to your business than others.

Please take the time to do this to the point where you feel very secure with such figures. The figures for any station will change somewhat with each survey. But if you have a pretty good idea of the audience for any specific station, you will not be over-awed by increases or decreases, normally brought to your attention by an announcement (usually on station letterhead) which looks like the example on the following page:

Figure 18. Radio station announcement.

Translation: OQQQ has more women age 55+ listening between twelve midnight Sunday and 5 a.m. Monday than any other station. Of course, the total number of women that age listening may not reach five hundred, so you may be buying a total audience of, say, one hundred women over the age of fifty-five. Whoopee.

Beware of such announcements. When a new survey comes out, call a friendly media rep and ask to see the book. In very few cases will there be so drastic an audience change that you should immediately change your media plan.

How to "Fly by the Seat of Your Pants"

There is another facet of media buying that can be fascinating. Provided that you are buying within your own immediate geographical area, you can (after you have gained experience and familiarity with the media) learn how to use your instinct in some cases.

This method lets you move with trends before the trend shows up in the survey. For example, suppose everyone you know starts watching a specific television show, and everywhere you go, people are commenting on it. Suddenly, you notice that your competitor's ad is showing up there. It's a pretty good bet that your competitor heard the talk, and is guessing that the audience for that particular show is growing fast. The survey to back up this hunch may not be out for six months.

Listen to radio, watch television, read that new column in the paper, and listen to the talk around town. Check with your favorite rep for that media. Use your own judgement and intuition. But, go very carefully with this type of buying, and don't try it at all until you are absolutely sure you know where the audience normally is in your area. Pay particular attention to those people who make up your target audience. And be sure you don't base any decision on your personal likes and dislikes.

What To Do If There is No Survey

Do your own. Hire a few high school seniors or juniors. Have them (a) stand in the local shopping center, or (b) telephone every third person (or pick your own method) in the phone book, and ask these (or similar) questions:

1. What radio station do you listen to?
2. Who is your favorite disc jockey?
3. What is your favorite television show?
4. How many newspapers do you read daily?
5. What time of day do you watch TV? Listen to radio?
6. What is your approximate age range (18-24, 25-35, 36-49, 50-65)?

Make sure the "helpers" you hire are polite, clean, neat, and intelligent enough to obtain the information you seek. Try working through the business class at the high school. Keep your list of questions as short as you can. Decide on a brief introduction for the surveyors to use, such as: "Hi! I'm (name). As an assignment for the business class, I'm taking a survey. Would you help by answering a few questions?" (or whatever spiel you can come up with).

Your goal is to obtain a reasonable size sample. If your city has more than 500,000 residents, try for around 300 to 500 completed cards. It may take you a week or two, and you may have to pay your helpers the minimum wage, but you should be able to glean some very interesting and helpful information. Besides this, you will be supporting the school system, and giving a group of young people the opportunity to learn something.

Once you have some idea of who is listening to or reading what, you will be able to apply the knowledge to your media buying plans.

Media buying is not tricky. It is a matter of finding out where your target audience is, and then placing your advertising as squarely in front of that audience as you possibly can. In the next chapters, there will be discussions of the separate media, and you will learn what to look for and how to buy.

Glossary of Terms

Before we go on to the specific media, there are some terms used in advertising that you should know. Don't try to learn them by heart (I'm not giving an exam!) but do read them over until you have some familiarity with them. Most of them are a kind of shorthand, or jargon, or technical language which does not seem to have penetrated as far as the dictionary. As a result, this book may be the only place you'll ever see them defined, though you will hear some of them quite a bit. The definitions are generally those agreed upon by usage.

Adjacencies   Commercials placed next to certain programming, such as news, weather, or sports.

Affidavit   Notarized statement that commercials were aired at certain times. Needed for co-op advertising.

Agency Commission   The 15% of a media buy allowed to recognized advertising agencies. That is, if a commerical price is listed as $100, an agency buying for a client would pay the station $85, and bill the client $100, thus deriving a 15% commission. If the client buys direct, he/she still pays the full $100.

Announcement   A commercial or "spot."

Air Check   A tape made of a commercial at the time of airing.

Availabilities   Frequently referred to as "avails," these are unsold time slots where commercials can be placed.

BTA   Best Time Available. The station schedules spots at the best time available. Spots bought on this basis are normally less expensive than those which are bought within a specific time period.

Bulk Plan   A plan whereby a retail business commits to buy a certain number of spots within a calendar year, earning a lower rate per spot.

Campaign   Planned advertising.

Cart(ridge)   A cartridge case containing ¼″ audio tape. These are used by radio stations.

Cassette   Audio or video tape in a case.

Commercial   Radio or TV ad.

Continuity   Scripts for commercials. Also, the department in a station which handles the scheduling of commercials.

Co-op   Time/space advertising cost shared by a manufacturer and a retailer.

CPM   Cost Per Thousand—cost to reach 1,000 people.

Copy   Either the written material inside a print ad, or a script to be read by an announcer.

Cume   Cumulative audience. Audience reached by a station over an extended period, usually a week.

Dayparts   Division of the broadcast day, radio.

Daytime   Television term, usually from eight or nine in the morning to four or five in the afternoon on weekdays. Sometimes used to refer to the period from 10 a.m. to 3 p.m. on radio.

Disc Jockey (dee jay)   On-air radio person.

Drive Time   Also "traffic time." Radio dayparts when listeners drive to and from work, usually six to ten in the morning and three to seven in the evening.

End Rate   The lowest rate at which a station offers commercial time for sale.

Evening   A radio daypart, usually 7 p.m. to 10 p.m., or 7 p.m. til midnight.

Fixed Position   A spot run at a guaranteed time, such as 8:05 a.m., for which a higher rate is paid.

Flight   A specific short term campaign on radio or TV.

Format   Kind of programming a radio station runs.

Frequency   Usually, the average number of times a person is reached by an advertising message within a specific time period.

Frequency Discount   Allowed when specific numbers of commercials are bought within a defined period, normally seven days.

Fringe   Television term for the times immediately before or after prime time.

Housewife Time   Radio (also TV) term for the hours from 10 a.m. til 3 p.m.

ID   Identification.

Jingle   A musical signature used for identification.

Live/Live Copy   Any commercial read by an announcer while he/she is on the air; not pre-taped.

Log   Station record of times commercials were aired.

Make-good   A spot run at a later time to make up for a spot missed or incorrectly run.

Midday   10 a.m. to 3 p.m.

Minutes   60-second commercials.

Open End   A recorded commercial which provides time at the end of the spot for a retailer's "tag."

OTO   A spot running One Time Only in a special program, normally television.

Package   Radio or TV—a combination of spots run within a specified time, offered at a special price.

Pre-empt   To replace a regular commercial or program. TV spots (or radio) bought at a low rate can be pre-empted by another advertiser paying more.

Rates   The charges for advertising time or space.

Reach   The number of different individuals reached in a given time period or combination of time periods.

Reel to reel   Using two separate reels of tape for recording.

Remote   A broadcast from a place other than the station's own studio.

ROS   Run Of Schedule (station)—same as BTA.

Schedule   Dates and times of day an advertiser's spots run during a specific campaign.

Spot   A radio or television commercial.

Share   The percent of listening audience tuned in to any one station at a given time.

Tag   An announcement at the end of a recorded commercial. Also, music at the end of live copy.

Talent   A performer on radio or TV.

Tape   Noun: magnetic tape for recording upon. Verb: to record a commercial.

TAP   Total Audience Plan. A combination of spots in each time classification which hit all of a station's listeners in a given time span, usually a week.

TF/TFN   Until Forbid, Till Further Notice—an ad schedule with no fixed end date.

Traffic   Department in an agency or station which sees that spots are run correctly.

Vertical Saturation   Running commercials heavily on one or more stations for one or two days.

Videotape   Two-inch tape used for recording television commercials. Also, ½" to ¾" tape for the same purpose.

There are other terms, of course. I have tried to include those most frequently used. If a rep uses a term you have never heard, don't be afraid to ask what it means. In fact, write it down and ask several of your reps. One of them may really know the meaning! (In some cases, I've found they will spout off terms and meanings without knowing what they are talking about.) It is an unfortunate circumstance, but it seems that media sales is a tricky profession. The guy calling on you from Station A today may be with Station C next week, and the lady at Station B may be someone who sold shoes until two months ago. A media rep who has been with one station for a measureable length of time (a year or two) is probably doing something right, and may know what he/she's talking about.

When you're buying media, don't trust anyone until they're proven trustworthy. Look at the facts instead of letting yourself be over-persuaded. It's your money. Spend it where the facts tell you you're likely to obtain results.

Chapter 5
The Art Of
Newspaper Advertising

Newspapers have a very specific place in the advertising budget. Before we get into the "how's" of using them, let's talk about the "why's."

A newspaper ad, or campaign, can be a good investment for a small business for several reasons.

Circulation

The first is "reach." Reach is the number of people, or households, who receive the paper. Normally, a newspaper will be received daily in a large percentage of the households within a given geographical area. If your budget is a small one, you can use small ads on a regular basis. If they are well-designed and well-placed, you will probably be able to attract attention to your business.

However, even if your newspaper sales rep is very persuasive, it is a good idea to check circulation figures before you commit dollars to newspaper ads. There is a factor most reps don't mention. No matter how many people receive the paper, you still have no idea how many of them will actually read your ad. Since you can assume that only a percentage will do so, it is wise to be sure that enough people receive the paper to make it probable that a reasonable number will see and possibly read your ad. If a paper has a circulation of 50,000 homes in a city of 500,000, the number of those people likely to read your ad is probably lower than if the newspaper had a circulation of 350,000 homes. Be sure the "reach" is as large as possible.

The Chance to Tell the Whole Story

The second reason for using a newspaper as part of your media planning is the ability it gives you to put down (in black and white) full information about your store, products, or services. It allows you to list items and prices, and to describe the items with words and pictures. It permits you also to give full and explicit directions to a location, up to and including a map, if one is necessary.

Reader Perception

The third reason is time. If a good prospect reads your advertisement, he/she can take all the time needed to read it, absorb it, look at it again. It puts your name, address, and telephone number in the reader's hands, to be used at the reader's convenience.

All of these are good reasons for considering newspaper advertising. There are also a couple of reasons to be a bit wary. One is the tendency of some people to read an ad only if they are ready to buy. For instance, if a man is ready to buy tires, he will notice (and probably read carefully) any ad dealing with tires. A person looking for a home will be likely to read the real estate section, or classified section, listing homes for sale. Of course, a well-designed ad that points out a special value or super sale will probably be glanced at by a large number of readers. But they will read the entire ad if they are really interested.

What the Surveys Can Tell You

Before you go too far with planning your newspaper ads or campaign, try to see a STARCH survey. If one has not been done in your city, try the largest city close by, or a rep from your largest radio or television station. The STARCH survey provides all sorts of information. For instance, ad size is a factor in readership, but it is not necessarily true that the larger the ad, the more readers it will have. The survey can give you ideas about the effectiveness of color in an ad, and how placement of the ad on a page can affect the readers.

The information is available, but you may have to dig for it. It's worth doing, because it can save you some money. There is no need to buy a full page ad if a quarter page will be just as effective.

Generally speaking, the advantages of using newspaper advertising outweigh the possible disadvantages, particularly if you are also using other media and newspaper is supportive. However, keep in mind that your newspaper ads should always be carefully designed and carefully placed. They should have a specific purpose, and should run with the right amount of frequency to accomplish that purpose.

Advertisement Placement

Newspapers in some cities will be cooperative in trying to place your ad where you think it will do the most good. In some cases, you may be able to pay extra and obtain exactly the placement you want. In most cases, a request to your rep should at least get you some consideration. Below are some sections or pages with possibilities for effective use by various kinds of businesses. For your own purposes, remember to keep your target audience always in mind.

Main News.
This section can be used to advantage by many kinds of businesses. Most people at least skim it, since (presumably) this section is why they buy the paper. A partial list of users includes: carpet dealers, automobile dealers, real estate firms, hardware stores, garden shops or florists, jewelers, furniture stores, clothing stores, department stores, tire dealers, grocery stores, home entertainment stores, appliance stores. The list is a long one. Almost anyone can place an ad in the main news.

Women's Pages (or Home Section)
A good place for ads directed toward women, including: bridal shops, photographers, gift shops, clothing stores, department stores, jewelers, gourmet cookware, children's items, book stores, men's gift items, furniture stores.

Financial or Business Pages
Excellent for advertising automobiles, real estate, men's clothing, office furniture or supplies, gifts for women, self-improvement courses for business people.

Sports
Items such as home video equipment, automobiles and accessories, men's clothing, sporting goods or clothing, sporting events.

Entertainment
Theatres, concerts, records, music stores, special events, home video or

stereo equipment are examples of businesses or items that can be advertised here.

These are some possibilities. Some of them are very obvious choices that have been proven successful. There can be a good deal of advantage, too, in moving an ad that seems to be a "natural" for one section, into another. For instance, a good real estate ad for an "executive home" with picture and descriptive copy doesn't necessarily have to go in the real estate or classified section. Why not put it in the business page, or the financial page, normally read by business people, and almost certainly read by those who are moving up and achieving executive status? Someone who has just been promoted (with salary raise) might be interested in moving up to a house that suits the "dignity" of the new position.

Talk to your newspaper rep, or the manager of the advertising department at the paper. Be frank about your target audience and ask for suggestions on new ways to attract their attention. If the rep has been keeping up with research figures, and paying attention to new ideas and trends, he/she should be able to give you some valuable assistance.

In addition, check surveys for percent of readership of certain pages for ideas on where to place your ads. Otherwise, think about what you are selling, and to whom you are selling it. A little effort on your part, and familiarity with your paper, will probably allow you to select the best place to put your ads.

Designing the Advertisements

When you buy newspaper space, what you have purchased is exactly that—empty space. It is up to you to fill the space with an effective message. To do this, you must carefully plan every word or picture that goes into the ad, and then lay the words and pictures out in the best way possible.

The basic term used in describing this is "layout." Layout consists of assembling a number of items in an advantageous way within a given amount of space. That definition is my own (and may appear to be an oversimplification), but it is workable for our purposes.

You have probably seen, or heard of, the method of figuring out whether your present furniture will fit the rooms in your new home. The idea is to draw a floor plan of the house to scale, then measure your furniture and cut pieces of paper to represent the furniture, to the same scale. You can then move the pieces of furniture around on the floor plan and see whether they fit, or where they fit best. Designing a newspaper ad uses somewhat the same technique.

We will discuss the technique more fully in a moment. Before we go any further, spend an hour or two with two or three issues of your paper. Look at the ads. Really look at them. Note which ones attract and hold your attention easily. Glance at location on the page, and try to decide how much this factor influenced you. Check the different type styles used, and the way various advertisers have made use of art, or of pictures of products. See the differences between regular ads and "reverse" ads (white type on black background).

Cut out five ads of various sizes which you really like. Cut out five ads that you dislike. Try to decide (as objectively as possible) what it is you like or dislike about them. This exercise will give you some idea of things you want or don't want in your own ads, though your taste isn't necessarily the most important factor. There are some rules it is advisable to follow for any advertisement.

In every ad which leaves your business, it is wise to follow the old journalism rule, and tell *who, what, when, where,* and possibly how or why.

The headline should be one that stops the reader. It should capture attention, and draw the reader into the ad.

Body copy (the rest of the words in the ad) should be concise, interesting, and to the point.

Prices, photographs, and illustrations should be used with specific purposes in mind. All illustrations should be used to show products, especially if your ad budget is small (meaning that your ads must be small). You don't need a bird in one corner if your headline says in large letters that you are having a "SPRING SALE!" Keep your ads simple.

The name, address, and logo of your business should be prominent. The hours you are open and your phone number should be included.

It is a good idea for all your print ads to have some relationship to each other, particularly if you are not running them very frequently. This relationship can be created even if you are using only type from the newspaper with your own name and logo. The examples on the following page will give you some idea of how this can be done.

**Figure 19. Here, the name (used as a logo)
and the reverse block have been used to help create
and maintain an identity.**

There are other ways, too, to make your ad stand out a bit from others on the page.

Reverse. Reverse is white type on a black background. A reverse block within an ad, or a totally reverse ad, can draw the eye of the reader, particularly if all the other ads on the page are regular.

Headlines. Somthing as simple as "Thank You!" leading into a sale ad can be effective. Try to be catchy, without getting "cute." Use a line or phrase that tells something significant—who, what, when, where, why— are always good standbys. Another point to keep in mind is the fact that you are paying for every single word in the ad, and are expecting every word in the ad to bring you a result. Use them carefully.

White space. This is a large area of white surrounding your message. It can give it distinction—even a look of "class." Unless you are a grocery store, or chain store, an ad that is crammed to the edges doesn't necessarily attract more readers. These kinds of stores normally have a large number of items, prices, and coupons, so patrons will go over them carefully to find the bargains on items they already use. The technique can be used by other businesses, of course, but in many cases, use of an ad filled to the brim with items and prices will tend to look like a grocery store ad. The two spaces below, designed differently using only lines, will give you some idea of how an ad looks either crammed full, or alternatively, with use of white space.

Figure 20. Use of White Space.

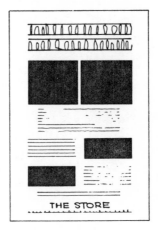

Unexpected appearance. You can achieve this by using something as simple as a letter to your customers, on letterhead, surrounded by a nice white space. You could then follow-up the ad with a letter to those customers already on your books. Or, a handwritten advertisement can be used. Most ads are set in type, so anything handwritten is certainly unexpected. A word of caution about this: Be sure every single word in your ad is easily read.

Borders. Most newspapers will have a selection of borders from which you may choose, or you can have your artist design a special border for your exclusive use. Such a special border can become an important contribution to the overall appearance of your ads, much as your logo will.

Look at those ads you have cut out of the paper. Notice the borders, the use of reverse, if any, the type styles. You should be beginning to have some ideas about what you like and dislike, and about the kind of appearance you would like your advertisement to have.

Further Tips on Designing Ads

Remember what we said about when you buy newspaper ad space that is exactly what you bought—space? If you have decided to buy an ad, sit down and draw yourself some space. Your newspaper may have layout sheets available to make this job easier. If not, you can start by measuring the column width in your paper, and using one inch to represent each fourteen lines in depth. For instance, if you have bought a 300-line ad, you can use two columns of width × 150 lines deep, or three columns × 100 lines deep, or four columns × 75 lines deep.

Some papers have rules about depth and width of ads. Be sure to check with your rep before deciding which format you will use.

Unless you are doing all the work yourself, and know what you're doing, there are basically two ways of doing newspaper ads. The first is to call in your artist, discuss the ad, and let the artist do the mechanical art, which you then send to the paper. The second way is to send the newspaper a layout and let them set the ad for you. The use of an artist will probably cost you a bit more, but has the advantage of assuring you that your ad will look exactly as you want it to look. You will also have an unlimited choice of type styles.

Newspapers normally have a selection of various styles from which you may choose, but if very many businesses are using the newspaper service, every advertisement will eventually begin to look like every other ad. This problem can be overcome to some extent if you will have your artist set key words in special type for your use in ads. You can then use these key words in your ads in conjunction with the newspaper service, thus giving your ads an individual appearance at a fairly minimum cost.

Whether your artist or the newspaper is setting your ad, you may want some "pictures" to break up the possibly dull look of all type, or to show special items. Again, you have some choices. You may use photographs, or line art, or "clip" art.

Photographs can certainly be effective. You may have black and white glossies available from your wholesaler, or you may hire a photographer to shoot special pictures for you. If you don't already know a professional photographer, check with your artist. Don't try to do it yourself, or let an amateur friend do it (unless you are sure the photographs will be of professional quality). Hiring a photographer can be expensive, so before you decide this is what you want, or need, check prices. Discuss with your artist or newspaper rep the possibility of using one of the methods below.

Line art is just what it sounds like. Glance through your paper again. You'll probably see many examples of line art. Usually, you must provide your own art to the paper for reproduction in your ad, unless a staff artist is available to assist you.

Clip art is art which is available through a service. Check with your newspaper rep on the availability of clip art to use in your ads. It is normally inexpensive, and if your budget does not permit use of original line art or photographs, use of clip art can be a way out. Sometimes manufacturers of products you are advertising will provide artwork.

If you are just beginning, and don't have the slightest idea what to do, first check with your manufacturer or wholesaler. Many companies have ad formats or slicks available for use by retailers. These have all the product information, even pictures, already laid out. They normally require a price, and the retailer's name and address, for which space is left open. These can be very helpful if you have absolutely no other choice. They will certainly let the public know that you have the item for sale, but they do nothing to establish an image for your store. The best way you can use them is probably to cut out and use those portions of the slicks you need, adding to this the information and logo and borders you are using to make your ads stand out.

If you are ready to design your advertisement, but don't have the least idea how to begin, try this step-by-step approach:

1. Gather all the facts you think you want in the ad. List them in descending order of importance.

2. Ask your newspaper rep to bring a "layout person" to a meeting. If this isn't possible, call your artist. Even if you want the newspaper to do the actual layout, you might ask your artist for comments. You may like the artist's ideas better than your own, and will probably need assistance with any special type you wish to use.

3. If you want to use a picture of some kind, at least write down a description of it, if one is not available. You will need to let the artist or layout person know exactly what you have in mind.

4. Decide what your headline should tell the reader. (**Gigantic Tire Sale! Learn To Type! New Spring Styles! Great Gifts For Mom!**

Lovely Carpet!) You can't use a single ad to tell a reader everything you would like to say about your business. You *can* attract attention to a specific (a sale, a service, your image), and once your customer comes in, show the rest of it. After you have established the main purpose of your advertisement, look at the list you made in Step One. Some items may have to be omitted, if your ad is not to look cluttered. The newspaper rep and/or your artist should have some suggestions on (for instance) the type styles which would look best and accomplish your purpose. From this point, listen to them.

5. Lay the ad out in the proper sized block, being certain that the most important item is prominent. Be sure that your name, address, and logo are in positions of importance.

6. Let the newspaper, or your artist, set the ad. If your artist sets it, and does a mechanical, once you have checked for errors, all you then do is get it to your rep for reproduction. If you use the newspaper, be sure to get a "proof" of the ad prior to the day it will actually run in the paper. Go over the proof carefully for spelling, and be certain that all the items and prices are correct. Look at it critically to be sure the items which are supposed to be attention getters look the way you think they should. Be sure the type chosen is appropriate, clear, and easy to read. Correct any errors now. An incorrect price can cause you a lot of hassle you do not need.

There are "good" and "bad" newspaper ads, of course. The good ones pull traffic into your store, the bad ones don't. Unfortunately, there is very little way to tell one from the other until you have run it. If you follow the rules, and create a nice looking, clean ad which contains a good lead line, copy that sells the reader on the benefits of whatever you're selling, and presents him/her with the facts needed to judge those benefits, as well as the facts about where to buy, you've done as much as you can.

The eight advertisements that follow illustrate what has been said fairly graphically. Take time to look at them carefully and read the copy. See if you can see for yourself what it is that makes them effective or ineffective.

Figure 21.

The headline, set off nicely in an invitational form, says what, who, when, where and why. The picture of the author, since he is "world-famous," should attract attention. The brief description of the book informs anyone who doesn't know already exactly what the book is about, and why they should buy it—after all, 200,000 people have already done so. The closing paragraph adds a hint of urgency, and gives an excellent suggestion for use of more than one personally signed book. The logo type of the store is clear and appropriate, and the border ties the ad together. The total layout is kept simple, with enough white space to give the ad a "classy" look and make it easy for a glancing look to tell the reader what is going on.

This ad, although it would probably be less expensive, also would not attract the attention of the version above. The copy is dull, and the headline has no excitement. The headline does not tell the pertinent facts 'who, what, when, where, why'—the entire ad must be read to discover who and what James K. Smith is. The body copy is difficult to read, due to the type style and the blocky look. *If* the reader was aware of the book and the author, he might realize what the ad is telling him. If he was not familiar with the book, there is

Figure 22.

James K. Smith will be in town Monday, July 13, to autograph copies of his latest novel, From Here to Mars in a Blimp. Be sure to stop by Remarkable Books and pick up your copy, and chat with this famous author.

REMARKABLE BOOKS
1111 Main St. 000-0000

nothing to make him even read the ad. The layout is static and uninteresting.

These two ads show how a little imagination can greatly help the appearance and content of your ads. A little money spent to make the ad an effective size may well pay for itself several times in the traffic it generates. In this case, however, even if the ads used the same amount of space, and were laid out exactly as they are here, the ad on the left would still be much better than the blocked, dull version without an effective headline on the right.

Bridal shops are selling tradition and beauty and memories. With that in mind, glance at these two ads.

Figure 23.

This ad does have a headline, and the body copy is certainly short and to the point. However, the overall effect of the ad is dull, and the tone is cold. There is nothing here to appeal to the prospective bride, unless she is primarily concerned with price alone. This is not usually the case, so the ad would not have mass appeal among engaged girls. The bad type style for the bridal shop name adds nothing, and the owner has forgotten to include address and phone number.

> **Juliet Bridal Shop is having a SALE!**
>
> **Save up to 16% on gowns.**
>
> Sample sizes 5, 7, 9.
> SOME MOTHER OF BRIDE SELECTIONS.
> 2 DAYS ONLY.
>
> **Juliet Bridal Shop**

In this ad, the headline immediately says that the shop is concerned with the same things a prospective bride is–making the wedding day a very special occasion. The body copy is interesting, the general style adds to the feeling of friendly, helpful service and concern. The shop knows that price is not the most important concern for the bride, but since it has some sample gowns it needs to move, the special sale is advertised tastefully, and given special emphasis through use of the little invitation card. The logo type for the shop is appropriate and the address and phone are clear. Any girl who wants hers to be a "wedding to remember" would be inclined to read this ad. From it she would not only glean the sale information, but also the fact that the shop can help with other aspects of the wedding. Again, with a little imagination, and a little more space, the shop has accomplished far more than telling only of a sale.

> **A Wedding to Remember**
>
> It's yours! And of course you want everything to be perfect. We'll be glad to help, with gowns, veils, invitations, photographs, flowers, and catering. We do it all . . . the way you dreamed of having it. We make it easy for you to have a perfect day, a wedding to remember with joy.
>
> **SAVE UP TO 16% ON OUR ENTIRE STOCK OF SAMPLE GOWNS FOR BRIDES AND MOTHERS. MANY STYLES TO CHOOSE FROM.**
>
> **Juliet Bridal Shop**
> 000 MAIN ST.-000-0000

Figure 24.

These two ads should give you a view of why it is usually better to be specific in your ads than general, and how you can use product illustrations to good advantage.

Figure 25.

The entire ad is designed to give the impression of a home, without being too "cute." If you read only the headline, you have all the pertinent information.

Who–Happy Hardware/home improvement headquarters.

What–A spring (home) fix-up sale.

When–is having now.

Why–you'll save money.

Where–Happy Hardware/address at bottom if needed.

The body copy and illustrations show several different kinds of "fixing-up" that can be done around most homes, from decorations to repairs. The prices are an attraction, and the store has included, in a separate block, a necessary item (paint) on sale at a very attractive price, with a special deal included. This kind of traffic builder can work nicely. Also, several different items, at several price ranges, gives the impression that the store has almost anything you might need to fix-up your house.

In this ad, on the other hand, although the store has made an effort with the reverse blocks, the copy is too general, the items on sale don't stand out, the picture of the outside of the store offers no incentive to the reader, and the inappropriate type style might even cause the ad to be totally overlooked. If you will look at these two ads carefully, and read them over for points we have discussed, you will see why one is so much more effective than the other. Even though they take the same amount of space, the difference in content should make a big difference in the amount of traffic they pull. This is the type of thing to keep in mind when you are designing your own ads.

Figure 26.

Here are two ads for the lighting design store. We have reduced the smaller-looking ad to make it fit the page, but in reality, it would be approximately the same size as the good ad. In this case, the effective ad has much more imagination and information than the bad ad.

Figure 28.

Here we have an example of a very static layout. The ad has very little, if any, visual interest and is quite dull looking. The headline would attract only those people already in the market for lamps. The illustrations are fine as they go, but certainly do little to show off the lamps to best advantage. Again, you can see how choice of logo type is important. In this case, using the "bad" type we previously discussed is obviously a bad choice. It can hardly be read at all. The only copy in the ad says nothing of real interest.

Figure 27.

Now, compare this ad with the one above. The layout is designed to draw the eye into the ad. The headline is interesting, and says who, what and why, as well as making a simple suggestion that might appeal to a wide number of people. Each of the copy blocks suggests an effective and attractive use for the merchandise, and again, the layout contributes to creating the beginnings of a picture in the readers mind. The list of specific fixtures and services, set off by bullets, is far more effective than a simple line saying "we have everything." Even the border in this case is more effective than the one above, since it becomes part of the design of the ad.

Timing Your Advertisements

The problem is this: you can run a great ad in the paper on a Sunday morning and pull no traffic at all. Or you can run a thrown-together version meant only to fulfill your lineage obligations on Wednesday evening, buried on a page with several other ads, and fill the store to overflowing. Readership of any one ad cannot be predicted. If you've studied a STARCH report, you should have some idea of how size, position, layout, and even color, can affect readership. You will have planned your ads accordingly, within the limits of your budget and goals. You will have created the best ad you could, being sure to tell your readers why they will benefit from buying a product or visiting your store.

However, your traffic may depend not on your ad, but on the weather! Or on the speech the President made on television the night you ran your ad! Or on a newscast that indicates a widespread flu epidemic is about to strike! Many different factors can affect the traffic you get from an ad. You can run the ad today and have not a soul in the store, and run the same ad at the same time next week and fill your store.

You Can Write Great Ad Copy!

Even if you've never written a word in your life; even if you have no idea of where to start, you can write good ads for your business. Here's how.

1. Keep in mind that the main purpose of every ad is to *sell*. Don't be clever for the sake of cleverness. Don't try to create an arty ad that will win prizes. Decide on a primary goal for each ad—that is, what the ad is selling—and be sure every word, picture, or line of type in the ad is *aiding* that goal.

2. Be honest. As a small business, you must establish and maintain a credible image. If you make a claim, you must substantiate it. Don't exaggerate. Don't make promises you can't keep.

3. Be sure to tell your consumer *why* he/she should visit your store, buy your product, or use your services. Be specific. Don't say, "We offer great service." Say, "We park your car for you; we carry out your packages; we have a playroom with a trained nurse to care for your child while you shop." Your consumers do not care why you think your product is great. They only care to know how it will be of benefit to *them*.

4. Write a headline that quickly and simply tells your customer how he/she will benefit. To do this, decide on the primary reason why customers would buy a product or come into your store. Will it save them time? Money? Work? Will it make their spouses love them more? Will it make their kids "A" students? Will it give them a chance to be President of their companies? Whatever the benefit is, make your headline one that tells it.

5. Write body copy that elaborates on the benefit(s). Keep this copy simple, direct, and concise. Some experts claim that you need extensive copy to sell. See what works best for you. Use the length you need to say everything important.

6. Tell them plainly what you want them to do. Tell them where and how to do it. Tell them when to do it, if that's important.

If you follow these guidelines, and if you take care with the layout and appearance of your ads, you should be able to accomplish your purpose. You should be able to create "good" ads.

If you still have doubts, try starting with the mats provided by your wholesalers, if you have them. Or go through your newspaper and read the ads carefully. You will begin to see that some of them attract attention to themselves, but not to what they are selling. Others make no impression in and of themselves, but leave you with a very clear idea that XYZ Store has your size tires on sale for three days only, at a $30 savings. This is the kind of ad you want to produce because it has made the right impression on you.

Here are some other ideas you may want to keep in mind:
1. Don't be afraid to poke a little fun at yourself. It makes you seem more human. If your competitor is three times your size, but you offer better service, play on this.
2. Don't sell general terms such as "We sell quality linoleum." Sell specifics. "Our linoleum is guaranteed not to stain. It's easy to wipe clean. It will last for ten years."
3. Be sure the product name and/or your store name is prominent and clear.

4. Remember that appeals to emotions and to status can be effective means of pulling traffic. "Be First..." "Be Best..." "Be Loved..." are used effectively every day.

Always, before you run a newspaper ad, decide on its primary purpose. Write your copy to fulfill that purpose. And remember, if you really have a problem, you can get help from your newspaper until you are more sure of yourself.

Whether you have ever run a newspaper ad or not, don't panic. Your newspaper rep will be glad to help. If the rep is unsatisfactory for any reason, you can always call the boss and ask for the assistance you need. If you are not happy with anyone at the paper, work with your artist and send the completed ad to the paper. Above all, don't forget to maintain your image (logo/type style/name/address) and identification in every ad. All of your advertisements, no matter what their primary purpose, should continue to build public awareness of your business.

Scheduling Your Advertisements

The frequency with which you use newspapers will be based on two things—your objectives, and your budget. If you plan to use newspapers infrequently, primarily as a tool to boost traffic during an occasional sale, your planning will be different than that of the person who is using the ads to build a constant image of a business. The latter will probably run ads on a regular basis, either weekly, or more frequently, as the budget allows.

Getting Discounts

If you are planning to run on a regular basis, check with your newspaper rep. Many newspapers will allow you a contract discount of from 5% to 15% of your lineage charges. This will depend on your willingness to agree to run a specified number of lines or inches per week (or per month) over a given period of time. If your paper allows such a discount, and you will be running enough ads to take advantage of it, do so by all means. Every dollar you save this way can be reinvested in another ad, or in radio, or other forms of advertising.

The size of your ads should be dictated by two things also. One, of course, is your budget. The other is the amount of information which must be included in a given advertisement. Use the size ad you need to tell the story. A full-page ad is not a necessity. A one-half-page ad will dominate a page. So will a quarter-page ad, if it is well-designed. On the other hand, don't let a slick-talking ad person talk you into using more space than you need. If you use quarter-page ads, and they pull all the traffic your personnel can handle, there is no need to run larger ads.

As in any of the media, the more frequently you run ads, the better-known you will become. Each time people notice or read your ad, awareness of your business grows. The likelihood of their remembering your name also grows, if they need or want what you sell.

Even if your budget is small and you run only one advertisement per month, try to use enough identity factors (logos, type styles) in each ad to remind people that they have seen your ads before. Every bit of awareness you can build will be of help in increasing your business.

Chapter 6
Radio In General

Radio is one of the best methods the small advertiser can use to reach the target audience. Here's why: most homes have one or more radios, most cars have radios, and many offices have radios. Radio is used as a companion by the homemaker and the long-distance driver, as a source of information and entertainment by almost everyone, and as background for many activities. Radio is generally not expensive to use, and reaches a large number of people at a low cost per thousand. With some careful forethought and planning, use of radio is within the budget of almost every small advertiser.

In recent years, radio has changed. With the advent of television programming (now available to most households), radio has deviated from dramatic programming to news, music, and specific public service or informational programs to meet the needs of varying audiences. Although most major media are now structured and planned to reach the prime buying public (18 to 49 years of age), radio is probably the most rigidly formatted.

Radio stations spend fortunes on programming research into the likes and dislikes of those people they wish to attract as audience. They then apply the results of the research to their programming. There are radio stations for the country music fan, for the rock music fan, for special ethnic groups, for teenagers, for pop music listeners, for news fans. There are programs aimed at truckers, at homemakers, at farmers. There are programs for those who are interested in current affairs, and those interested in religion. All this effort on the part of the radio stations makes your media-buying job a lot easier.

Due to their specialization, as a buyer you can easily zero in on those specific people or groups you most want to reach. You can allocate exactly the amount of money you need to reach those people, and with a little planning, check on your results. Also to your advantage is the fact that radio costs continue to rise more slowly than those of some other media. This makes radio a good buy and an efficient means of reaching your target audience.

Another advantage to radio is the fact that you can use it in a number of ways. You can make a direct one-to-one appeal to the listener. A good radio commercial can sound as though you are talking directly and exclusively to each separate member of the audience. You can use it to establish exactly the type of image you wish your business to have, through the selective use of audio images. These range from a simple announcement of a sale, to a complex multi-voice situation, to an identifying jingle, to the use of exactly the right background music or effects to complete a picture in the listener's mind. Radio is extremely versatile, and the production costs are usually far less than they are for television.

Radio Advertising

An advertisement for radio consists of audio only. You cannot buy a picture on radio. When you buy a radio schedule, you have bought a certain amount of time, which you must then fill with an effective combination of sounds that sell your store or product. The sounds range from the human voice, through special effect and music, to a combination of all of these.

The time for a commerical is strictly limited. You have exactly ten seconds, or thirty seconds, or sixty seconds in which to introduce your store or product, tell your audience why they need to buy the product or shop in the store, and how and where to do so.

These times you buy, called commercials or "spots," are in various time periods in the broadcast day. For instance, you may buy one 60-second spot every day for seven days on one radio station. That spot can be placed in the morning or afternoon drive time, in midday or homemaker time, in the evening, or during the all-night time. The specific placement of your spot is important, since the placement determines the audience size. Audience size determines how many people will be likely to hear your message.

Drive Time

Drive times are those times during the day when people drive to and from work. They are normally the hours from six to ten in the morning, and three to seven in the afternoon. Besides the normal nine-to-five worker, these times include the seven-to-three and three-to-eleven shift workers. The times allow the advertiser to reach the greatest number of listeners possible, since most people now have car radios. Many have them on during the drive to and from work.

Some careful research into the listening habits of the people in your city, when combined with your knowledge of your target audience, can tell you exactly when and where to place your spots to best advantage.

Midday Time

The "midday" or "housewife" times are generally from ten in the morning til three in the afternoon on weekdays. The audience on many stations is lower during these hours than during drive times. It is, for the most part, composed of different people. For instance, an AM station may show a drop in male listeners during these hours, and a change in the ages of the female listeners. On the other hand, an FM/ Easy Listening station may show a slight or even a major, increase in audience. This is because many offices have a radio on as background, and for the most part tend to want more music and less talking than is to be found on an AM station.

Also included in the radio day are the hours from seven in the evening until midnight, and midnight to six in the morning. Prices for commercials are generally lower on most stations during these two times. There are reasons for this.

Television begins to absorb the available audience during the early evening. The hours from eight to eleven are considered television's prime time. After eleven o'clock, particularly on weeknights, the available audience drops sharply, since most people go to bed. For these reasons, there are fewer people available to listen to radio, so the price per commercial usually drops.

A station which sells drive time spots for $60 a minute may well sell the seven-to-ten or midnight time at, say, $25 per spot, and the "all-night" or midnight-to-six in the morning for even less.

The cost of a commercial on a radio station is based primarily on the number of people listening during the time the commercial is aired. Of course, the stations from time to time raise prices to keep up with costs. This is so their profits remain at a viable level, but they cannot raise prices beyond the point justified by their audience levels. To do so is to price themselves out of business. Other factors influencing the rate structure are station popularity, selling power, and the size of the market.

Before you go any further with planning a radio buy, do some research on the stations in your area. To give you some idea of the facts you need to know to make a buy that will effectively reach your target audience, glance at the fictitious chart below. If your business is in a city or metro area of any size, this information (or a variation of it) will be available.

Station	Programming	Adults Reached 6AM-12M	Age Range	Broadcast Hours
A	MOR	115,000	34-49	24
B	Easy Listen.	45,000	35-65	24
C	Rock	108,000	13-25	24
D	Adult Contemp.	25,000	25-35	24
E	Country	32,000	25-49	Daytime
F	Album Rock	15,000	18-35	Daytime

There is a great deal more information than this available in most cities. However, from the categories above, we can obtain much useful information. Take a look at your target audience. Compare the age, and likely tastes of the people you are selling to with the above chart, and see if you can begin to decide where you might place your spots. You should be able to begin making a decision, although in a real buy, the information you obtain can be far more specific.

Another thing to consider, of course, is the cost of the commercials. Let's assume you can spend $200 on a schedule. There is a simple formula that will tell you which station is the most efficient buy, no matter what the price per spot is. The formula will tell you the cost per thousand listeners who can be expected to hear your spot, based on the figures available from the surveys. When figuring the CPM (cost per thousand), keep in mind that you are working with units of 1,000; that is, if the survey shows 115,000 listeners, you will be working with 115 units of 1,000.

$$CPM = \frac{\$200}{115} = \$1.74$$

This example, $200 schedule divided by 115 units of 1,000, gives an approximate cost per thousands of $1.74. Using the figures in the example above, try figuring out a couple of your own. This will give you a good idea of one way to decide on which station is the most efficient buy. This is if your only consideration in making a buy is reaching the largest number of people or the least cost. Obviously, it is not necessarily true that the less a spot costs, the better its value.

Many inexperienced or new advertisers tend to believe that if they can buy thirty spots on one station for the same price as ten on another station, the thirty-spot buy is the one to make. Again, considering numbers only, if the thirty-spot station reaches 8,000 listeners in a seven-day schedule, and the ten-spot station reaches 115,000, the ten-spot station is probably a better buy. Don't be fooled into buying "bargains" on a station with very few listeners.

However, there are many other factors to be considered before you make a buy. If, for instance, you are selling a very specialized item to a particular audience, and the audience who might be expected to buy the product listens only (or mostly) to the thirty-spot station in the example above, you would probably have to buy time on that station in order to reach them.

It should be becoming more and more obvious to you that in order to buy and use any advertising medium effectively, *you* must know *what* you are selling *to whom*. You must have a realistic profile of your customers. You must define your target audience, and then aim your advertising at that audience.

The Number of Spots to Buy

Once you have decided which stations are the best for reaching your audience, you must decide how many spots to buy. Most businesses have a limited advertising budget, so there is no possible way for them to cover every single station every hour of the day. However, in order to be effective, a radio spot must normally be heard more than once. Therefore, it does little good, either, to buy one spot on every station in town once a week. Only the "dial turners" (those people who switch continuously from station to station) will have any opportunity to hear the spot as much as twice, and that would be sheer luck.

Before we go any further, let's think for a moment about what you're trying to achieve through your use of radio. The frequency with which your spots are aired will be affected by what your goals are.

For any retail business, there are two basic kinds of advertising, which we have discussed before. The "image-building" ads, and the "special event" ads.

Image Building

In order to build image and public awareness of a business, a steady, small schedule will work to build the desirable frequency. You may, for instance, use four spots per week, two each on two different stations. As long as the spots run at approximately the same time each week over an extended period of time, an effective frequency will be established.

This is not to say that each time one of the spots runs your place of business will be jammed full of people. What should happen, if your spots are good, is that over this period of time, your name will become familiar. Then, if a person needs or wants the product or service you offer, your name should come to mind, hopefully more rapidly than the name of your competitor. The idea of this type of spot schedule is to use it in conjunction with your advertising in order to keep your name in front of your buying public during those times when you are not having a special event which requires a more intensive campaign.

Announcing A Sale

For the special event, or sale, you will probably wish to use a far greater frequency over a much shorter period of time, in order that as many as possible of your potential customers will be aware of the event. This can mean buying a number of spots on several stations for several days, in order to be as sure as you can that your target audience hears the spots two or three times. You might decide that your budget allows a three-station buy for two days—the day before the sale, and on the sale day itself. If your budget permits, you might want to schedule spots for two days prior, or even three, as well as on the sale day.

If all of this seems terribly confusing, don't panic. Call the media rep you befriended in Chapter Three. If your rep is helpful and cooperative, you can very quickly explain your problems. Your rep will be able to help you decide which stations in your market are your best buy for both kinds of schedules, as well as help you figure out whether the stations are an efficient buy for you. Many stations today have a computer service that will break down facts and figures into neat columns which make it easy for you to see both good and bad buys.

Don't hesitate to use every resource you can find. A media rep, if he/she is good, will be interested in being sure that the dollars you spend get results for you, since results are the one thing that will keep you buying.

In all fairness, try not to exploit the services of a rep from a station which can obviously never (or almost never) be a part of your planning. You should be able to find someone good from a station which you plan to use. In such a relationship, both of you will profit.

Rate Cards and Buying a Schedule

Most stations publish a rate card for local (or retail) advertisers. Such a card generally shows the station's established rates for ten, thirty, and sixty-second spots within the separate dayparts discussed earlier. Generally, there will be a small rate break for frequency, and the spots in the less desirable time periods will cost less. Some stations, whose audience levels remain approximately the same during the entire day, may have one basic price per spot, and vary the price only slightly according to how many spots you buy.

You will have to check your area and obtain rate cards from the stations you plan to use, and then learn to read the cards. Some stations use straight cards, others use a "grid" card which allows them to price spots at several different levels, and then charge according to how many spots are available for sale. Rate card structures are as varied as the stations, and some are very complex. Learn to read them before you plan to buy. If you have trouble figuring out what they mean, by all means consult with the rep.

Once you know which stations you will use, and have decided on your budget for a buy, you still have to decide where and when your spots will run.

You may find it easy to make a plan like this one:

Station	Date Thurs.	Date Friday	Date Saturday		
6-10AM	2	3	4	9 @ $___	= $____
10-3PM	2	3	4	9 @ $___	= $____
3-7PM	3	4	3	10 @ $___	= $____
7-10PM	2	3		5 @ $___	= $____

____ = Total, Station A

If you are making a three-station buy, for three days, this kind of plan will help you see just where your spots will fall. If you plan far enough in advance, you can probably get exactly the times you want, on the days that will be of most benefit to you. Your reps should be very willing to help you work up a schedule which meets both your needs and your budget. If the specific times your spots will run are very important, it is a good idea to call the rep in and buy your schedule three to four weeks in advance of the event you are advertising. This is because during some weeks the station(s) may be sold out of availabilities in the times you prefer. Unless you are running an "ROS" schedule, which allows the station to place your spots at its discretion, in return for a lower cost to you, and as long as you are paying the current rate, your contract date should prevent your spots from being pre-empted by another advertiser.

Do check with your reps for information on this type of thing, so that the day before your schedule starts you are not unpleasantly surprised to find out your spots have been moved to other times and days.

There is something else to keep in mind here. The number of commercial minutes within an hour of broadcast time is limited. Check with your reps if you have specific questions about this. For the most part, it helps to know that in busy times, on popular stations, commercial time can indeed be sold out. Be sure to plan ahead and buy your schedules as far in advance as you can.

Prime Rates

You should be aware, too, that stations sometimes offer two distinct types of rates. The first is the "Top of the Card" or "prime" rate. When you you buy a schedule at this rate, you contract for your commercials to run at specific times, and you will pay the station's top going rates. This means that if you want a spot to run from six to ten on Wednesday morning, it will run during those hours. Even more specifically, some stations allow you to request the exact time a spot will run, and for this they will charge a "premium" rate. Your spot should then run within that time.

Less Expensive Rates

Another option offered by the stations is the TAP (Total Audience Plan) or ROS (Run Of Station) schedule. This second type of buy allows you to run spots more cheaply, because it gives the station the option of moving your spots to another day or time, if necessary. A TAP plan is normally one in which your spots are scheduled to run in each of the dayparts, usually not including the midnight-to-dawn time. You might, for instance, buy ten spots a week on this plan. Within a seven-day period, your spots should run in all the times from six in the morning til midnight, thus theoretically reaching the station's total listening audience.

An ROS plan is usually less specific. If you buy ten spots a week, the station can run them wherever a time slot is open, with no guarantee that every time period will be used. Spots purchased ROS are usually the least expensive. But, unless you buy a large number of spots per week, you are not necessarily going to reach the station's total audience.

It is a good idea to talk with your reps about any such options available. You may find that a constant ROS or TAP plan, combined with a few spots in drive times, will give you exactly the audience you need.

Also, from time to time, stations will come up with and present special "packages" of one sort or another. These may be something as simple as a one-month bargain price on ROS spots, to a $5,000 three-month package which carries with it a trip to a foreign country or one of the more exciting cities in the United States.

This kind of package seems to appear during the "off seasons"— generally January and February, or perhaps July and August. Depending on your planning and budget for these months, the packages may or may not be of value. Don't sign up for them unless you are sure they fit your budget and can be of assistance in building toward your advertising goals. It is well to consider that a station may be offering such a plan in order to boost its business during a slow time, just as you might have a sale. The time they offer such packages is not necessarily the best time for you to buy them. A "free" four-day trip for you and your spouse to Acapulco can look marvelous and exciting, but don't buy it at the expense of your total ad budget for six months.

To summarize a bit, let's consider the basic things we have discussed. First, radio is an excellent medium for the small advertiser, if it is bought with careful attention to target audience and advertising goals, and if the budget is spent with the goals in mind. Be careful when buying radio not to be over-awed by a persistent media rep. Look at reputable survey figures, the station programming, and the type of people listening. Base your buys on these facts. If your town is a very small one, you may be better off doing your own survey than listening to what the reps tell you. This is especially true if they are basing their promotions on unknown survey materials. Try to be aware of WHO does the surveys, as well as being familiar with your city, before you lean too heavily on material presented by someone trying to make a sale.

Once you have decided on your goals and your budgets, try to plan as far ahead as you can, so that you can be sure your spots will run at the times which will be most advantageous to your business.

Last, but certainly not least, be sure your radio commercials are good, which is what the next chapter is about.

Chapter 7
The Radio Commercial

The Commercial

You've just made a $500 radio buy, to start in three weeks, and you are now faced with creating a commercial. You may be absolutely delighted to know that most radio stations will, if necessary, write your commercial for you. Either your rep, or someone else at the station may be available to take your facts and string them together into an acceptable spot. Each station you buy will create its own version of your facts for presentation on the air, sometimes even with music as background, or with special effects.

There may, or may not, be a small charge for this service, and the abilities of the people providing the service may or may not be good. If you absolutely cannot do it yourself, you may certainly use this service. If you do, be sure to request that you hear the final version of the spot *before* it goes on the air. To neglect this is to leave yourself open to all sorts of problems you really don't need. For instance, you should be sure all the facts in the commercial are correct, including the name of your business and the address, the hours you are open, and, of course, be sure any prices mentioned are accurate.

Before you decide this is what you want to do, let's look at the possibility of doing it yourself.

Writing a simple, straight commercial is not really very difficult, but there are several things you should keep in mind.

Writing the Commercial

First, sit down and list the facts that need to be included. The name and address of your business, the hours you are open, the dates of the sale (the "who, what, when, where, why and how"). These facts will tell a listener exactly what is going on. Then list the pertinent information about your particular event. You might include special prices, special dates, special items, or any other fact that is a basic piece of information you wish to get across to your target audience.

Once you have your facts in good order, you can begin to write the spot. Don't just sit down to write without making this kind of list. Until you have some experience in writing commercials, you are quite likely to leave out something as vital as the name of your business. This happens because you are very familiar with your subject, and it escapes your mind that your customers may not know which store in town is having the sale, until they are told.

Also, be sure you know how long your spots need to be. A thirty-second commercial runs about seventy-five to eighty words. A minute spot runs about 150 to 170 words. These are guidelines; you don't have to have this many words, and you can sometimes use more. But you should keep in mind how you want the commercial to sound. If you try to crowd ninety to 100 words into a thirty-second spot, the best announcer in the world may sound just a little more rushed than you'd like. (Actually, the announcer probably won't be able to take a breath from the first word to the last, and may sound like an express train gone crazy.) On the other hand, if you're trying to create a special feeling of excitement, you may use a few more words, or some music or sound effects, to try to give your spot a little extra push. Alternatively, if you are trying to create a feeling of beauty, or calmness, or luxury, you may want to use fewer words. Be very picky about the kind of music used as background.

If you have followed all the ideas listed on the next few pages, and your spot is ten words longer than the guidelines, try this. Read it over to yourself to get the feel of it. Then read it at *normal speed, out loud.* I don't mean yell, but read in a slightly higher volume than normal, being very sure to pronounce each word carefully. Time yourself as accurately as you can with a second hand or stopwatch. If you can comfortably read the spot within or close to the allotted time, you are probably not too far out of line.

The Professional Announcers

If the spot is written smoothly, a professional announcer can handle a few more words than you can—but not many. If you don't mind if the announcer sounds rushed, fine. If you want the commercial to sound relaxed, cut some words, or rewrite the spot. Many people who try to write copy for commercials try to crowd in every single fact they can dig up about a sale, and then wonder why no one understood the announcer. You will be far better off to use one or two selected items, tell about them, and make quite clear where and how to find them, than trying to list all the items included in the sale.

Once you have your facts listed, there are a couple of other rules you should bear in mind. Thirty seconds is a long time. A sixty-second spot seems to go on forever. Therefore, make it a rule to be sure the name of your store or business is mentioned several times in each spot. Three times in thirty seconds, four or even five times in a sixty-second spot, are a good idea.

There are exceptions, of course. In fact, there are legitimate exceptions to almost every rule of good copywriting. But until you know the rules, and can use them well, stay with them. After you learn them, you may break them. Until you do learn them, you may make serious mistakes if you disregard them.

What You Want Your Commercial To Do

If you have very firmly in mind the facts you want to include, and are aware that you will try to use your name the appropriate number of times, think about what you expect the commercial to accomplish for you. Are you having a big sale that should attract numbers of people? Should the spot sound exciting and enthusiastic? Are you trying to create a picture in the listener's mind, as might be the case in selling a particularly nice subdivision? Decide on a particular objective for your commercial, and try to decide how you might best convey your meaning to your audience.

For a sale, you might want to start your spot with a sound effect or music, and have the announcer come in over this with a very enthusiastic **"Sale, Sale, Sale! That's Right, _____ Is Having A Sale. This Thursday And Friday, You'll Find..."** This is a very simple approach, but it may be just what you need. If you use such an opening, or anything similar, be sure you remember to say who is having the sale several times. You may continue to use general terms, such as **"Inventory Closeout"** or **"Year-end Bargains"** and so forth, or you may list a particular item, give the sale price, or say, **"Save Up To $___."** Use any such thing you want, but do try not to confuse the listener with too many items and too many prices.

The idea of a good commercial is to let the target audience know what's going on, and then give an example that will entice him/her to come in and see what else is available. Do be sure *(ALWAYS)* to be honest about this. It doesn't make sense to get yourself in trouble with authorities by lying about your prices or the sale prices. Don't advertise items you don't have available, and don't misrepresent those you do have. Such tactics may crowd your store, but anyone who is disappointed or angered at being led on by falsehoods is not going to come back for more, and you may land in hot water!

When writing this type of simple spot, it's a good idea to think of several catchy lead-in lines, and try using them with several versions of the facts that need to be included. Always keep in mind that the commercial must be read aloud. It must move smoothly from one thought to the next. Below is an example of such a simple spot. There is nothing great about it, but it does include the pertinent facts. It does use the name of the business three times, and it does flow easily so that an announcer would have no trouble reading it correctly. The announcer can emphasize the important ideas, and have room to breathe every now and then. You will note there is a form to follow. Every station doesn't have the same idea as to how a commercial should be presented, but if you use this, or a similar format, they will probably understand what you want.

Type your spots (double-spaced) using all caps. Underline any words that need particular emphasis. Try to use complete sentences when you first start writing commercials. Later, you may be able to deviate from this a bit, but in the beginning it is probably better to strive for clarity and ease of understanding.

Figure 29. Script for radio commercial.

The Store

Title: Spring Sale

Length: 30 seconds

Effective: 5/15/-- **End:** 5/18/--

Sound Effects: Exciting, brassy music, with "marching" feeling. Establish 2-3 seconds, fade under announcer.

Announcer: Hear Ye! Hear Ye! **the store** is having a fantastic spring sale. March on down to **the store** and select your new spring and summer outfits at **terrific savings.** Choose bargains in skirts and blouses in bright spring colors or wash-and-wear suits starting at just $29 each. Don't miss the spring sale at **the store,** 2900 Park Avenue. Save til nine Thursday and Friday evening, at **the store,** your place for bargains galore on the latest spring styles.

This is a very simple spot, of the type that is used by many businesses every day. The business merely wants to convey to its target audience that there is a special sale going on, and to entice the audience to come in and see the bargains. The announcement at the beginning and the bright, brassy music serves to attract attention to the fact that this is a special event. The copy includes facts about when and where, and offers a price on one item which may serve as an attention-getter. It is not a difficult spot to write, even if you have no experience in stringing words together. If you will list the facts, and remember to include the name of your business, and then come up with a catchy lead line, the spot will almost write itself.

A couple of hints to keep in mind are the fact that the music or sound effect should contribute directly to the purpose of the spot. No lead line should be used for its own sake—it should lead directly into the purpose of the spot. That is, don't ask for "background music" unless you can at least describe the feeling you want the music to convey. Don't use a lead line that is totally unrelated to the spot. Keep in mind that the announcer has to read it out loud, and therefore, it should at least make sense.

Also, be sure everything is spelled correctly. If there are words (particularly proper names) that may have questionable pronunciation, show how it should be said. For instance, if your name is Macsen, write it out the way you want it said—as *"MACK SIN"* or *"McSIN"* or *"Mack SIN."* Don't get too complex, just try to make any unusual word clear to the announcer.

Another rule of thumb that many copywriters feel is wise is never to use a lead line which can be answered "no." Examples include:

"Looking for a used car?"
Listener's mental answer might be "no." End of spot.

"Thinking about a new home?"
NO—end of spot

Sometimes, of course, a leading question can be an effective way of getting attention. But until you're very sure of what you are doing, test your lead lines. If they can be answered "No," try to find another line, or another way of saying the same thing. Examples:

"If you're looking for a good used car,
now is the time to check out the values at ..."

"The homes in Lovely Lawns may be just
the right home for your family..."

This kind of commercial is perhaps the simplest use you can make of radio air time. If it is well-written, if it says what you want it to say, and does the job you want it to do, it can be as effective as any other type. However, there are a number of other types of commercials which you may want to consider using.

Sound Effects

Since radio uses sound, you may use pure sound to create the problem to which your product will be the solution. Let us suppose that you sell sound-proofing for homes or offices. Let's further pretend that you are trying to sell to a busy executive. You might then create a spot similar to this one:

Figure 30. Script for radio spot using sound effects.

Sound Effects: Traffic noise, establish loud, 4 seconds, add horn blowing, 2 seconds over loud traffic. As horn ends, fade traffic slightly, bring in siren sound in distance, slowly increase to full, then fade siren down and out (total siren 3½ seconds). traffic noise up slightly, church bell strikes nine times, then out. Street vendor shouts "Hot dogs, get your red hots here!" (bells and voice, 6 seconds total). Bring in distant train whistle, child crying, and adult voices, total 4 seconds, still over traffic. At 21 seconds, sound of door opening, man's voice, "Good morning." Woman's voice, "Good morning, sir." Door closes, ½ to 1 second of silence, then announcer tag.
"Buy yourself some peace and quiet. Call J and J Soundproofing, today."

This type of spot lends itself to a number of different businesses. Even if you sell something that at first glance seems soundless, think about it. You may come up with a way to use sound for your commercial instead of words. Radio stations usually have some sound effects available for use by advertisers. If they don't have the particular sound(s) you have in mind, check your local record store. Don't wait until the last minute to do so, since the record(s) you need may have to be ordered. As a last resort, you can buy or borrow a decent cassette tape recorder and microphone, and go out and find the sounds you need, and record them. This is a little more trouble than most people want to go to, but it can be done, if necessary.

The "Conversation" Commercial

The next type of spot you may want to consider is the "two-voice" or "conversation" spot. It is easiest to create and use this type of spot if you have sixty seconds. A thirty-second spot, using two voices, may sound very rushed. Again, be sure you have your facts straight. Then decide what you want the spot to accomplish before you start to write. Once you have done these two things, there is a further point to consider.

Two voices usually mean two personalities. Two personalities lend themselves to several kinds of feelings. Depending upon what you are selling, and the image you wish to create, you may choose to have the two people arguing, joking, asking and answering questions, simply discussing facts, or using some other technique.

Since two personalities probably mean that you will pay a "talent" fee, as well as possibly a fee for the use of a recording studio, it is a good idea to decide exactly how the use of two voices (or more) will be of benefit in creating the image you want to convey. Don't use two voices if one will do just as well. When you first start thinking about the spot you are writing, if an idea occurs to you that seems to require two voices, then is the time to consider it.

If you are selling a wine, for instance, and you want to tell people how great it is, you can have an announcer say that it is flavorful and goes well with meat and is a great ice-breaker. Or you can have two people discussing the delightful flavor, with the atmosphere suggested by background music and the clink of dishes and glasses and the intimate tones of voices, as if two people are in a restaurant enjoying the wine.

When writing copy for radio, always keep in mind that you are using SOUND—and USE it.

Use of a Jingle

Another type of radio spot involves the use of a jingle, or musical signature. Normally, you cannot produce this yourself, since most jingles use several singers and an orchestra, as well as, perhaps, an announcer. A jingle consists of music, singing, and sometimes copy that is spoken. In many cases, a jingle will begin with one to three seconds of music. The singers will then sing for ten to fifteen seconds. There will be a break of perhaps twenty to thirty seconds, during which the music continues in the background, then the singers will come in again and end the spot. That break in the middle is known as a "donut," and may be filled with any copy you desire.

Some jingles, known as "full sing" versions, have no donut, and the singing is continuous for the full length of the spot. In most cases, if you buy a jingle package, you should obtain thirty and sixty-second full-sings, and thirty and sixty-second versions with donuts. That way, you can use whatever is necessary to accomplish your particular purpose. Radio stations sometimes can help you obtain jingles through jingle houses. You may have a studio in your city which produces them. Perhaps you will be approached by someone who has created a successful package for someone in your business in another city, and is now trying to sell the package across the country. There are a couple of things you should keep in mind.

First, be absolutely certain that jingle you propose to buy will convey the proper image to your target audience. If it does not, no matter how clever it is, don't buy it. For example, if you sell a luxury item, and your audience is a very sophisticated one, it may not be wise to buy a jingle that has as its theme "___ has the cheapest prices in town." Also, since a jingle package can be expensive, you should be sure it is one you can use for a long period of time (at least a year, maybe more). Be very sure that the expense of the jingle doesn't mean you have no money left to put it on the air. A $5,000 package may sound great in your office, but if that $5,000 is the total ad budget for the next three months, it may not be a wise investment.

If you are interested in obtaining a jingle, check with your media reps for sources, and listen to several different kinds of jingles before you decide to buy. They can be very simple, or very complex. But the one you choose should exactly suit the image of your business which you are trying to convey to the world.

You should be aware, too, that a jingle is not an absolute necessity. If you are just starting in business, you may want to wait a while before investing in an item that should be used for several months or years. Many experienced people do not think that a jingle adds much to a spot, and prefer to be creative with copy and sounds. These are meant to convey exact images and meanings, rather than depend on the more generalized image created by the use of jingles.

Inexpensive Alternates

There are other ways to establish and maintain an audio image that may be used in place of an expensive jingle. Use of such an audio logo or signature is a good idea, since the small advertiser may not be able to afford to stay on the air constantly. If you have an audio logo, it will help people remember that they have heard from you before. These ideas are listed for your convenience. The thing to do is select one of these methods, then use it in all your radio spots.

1. Find an announcer you like, and pay his talent fee to record every one of your spots. After a bit, the voice will become your logo. This is a good idea, but do keep in mind that announcers don't always stay in the same city forever. You may have to change.

2. Find, or have a local service create a musical or sound logo. It should be brief, distinctive, and memorable. It should sound well used at the beginning or at the end of your spots, so you can vary its use.

3. Write yourself a logo line. It should be catchy and easy to remember. And short. "It's THE STORE—for bargains galore" is an example.

4. Create a logo line, as above, and put it with a sound effect or music for extra emphasis.

There are other ways, but these are simple ones that can be used by almost any small advertiser. Your reps may be able to help you find what you need. You may have to dig up a friend who plays the oboe, and ask him to help. Whatever you do, once you have established a logo, keep using it. After you and your staff are totally sick of it, after you are sure everyone in town is sick of it, keep using it.

Maintaining Your Image

Many people find and use a marvelous logo for six months, then change, just as the general public is becoming aware of it. If you have a good thing going, don't be in a hurry to change it. A good audio logo or jingle can be used effectively for long periods of time. Some have been used—literally for years.

"Other Resources"

If you have read all this, and still don't have the least idea where to begin, there are other sources that may be of help. Check with some of your radio reps to see if they have sample radio spots available for you to listen to. There are services which provide these ideas, along with the stories of how they have been used successfully. You should by no means try to use someone else's spot, merely substituting your name and address. However, if a business like yours has created and used a spot of some type, you can adapt that idea to your own use in your city. It is not a good idea to steal ideas anywhere, and particularly unwise to use any idea already in use by a direct competitor in your city. If the competitor used it first, your advertising using the same idea will probably sound like the competitor's advertising. Your ad will direct your potential customers to your competitor's place of business! Listening to many spots can sometimes trigger an idea for a spot for you, even though when finished, your spot will not sound like the original one.

Many radio stations across the country are members of the Radio Advertising Bureau, popularly known as RAB. Such stations can obtain cassette tapes of spots for many different product lines and businesses from RAB, along with information about how the spots were used, and why they were successful. If you would like to hear some spots that have worked for others in your field, check around to see if one of your local stations is a member. Your rep from that station should be able to obtain a cassette for you to listen to. You will find that many of the spots, however good they are, may not be appropriate for your image or goals. However, you should get some ideas that can be translated into commercials for your store or business. In any case, listening to successful examples of radio commercials can be of help in making you more aware of the many different ways radio can be used.

If all else fails you, sit down and listen to several of the radio stations in your area for several days. Even if you hate the music they are playing, you may begin to have some idea of the many varieties of commercials available for you to choose from. If you hear a spot you like, make a note of it, and why you liked it. If you hear an idea you like, make a note of it. Once you have these notes, sit down again with your list of information and think. What is the main idea you are trying to convey? Reduce that idea to one sentence, as concise and clear as you can make it. With that one sentence, and your list firmly in mind, you should begin getting some ideas for your spots.

This works easily when you are trying to come up with an idea for a commercial for a single event. Deciding on a spot or spots for a campaign to build image may be a little more difficult. In this case, you will perhaps have a list of four or five points you feel must be conveyed to your potential customers.

For this type of schedule, you will probably have fewer spots per week, spread over a long period of time. If this is true, try taking each of the points you wish to make and reduce it to a single sentence, as above. Then think of the atmosphere you wish to create, so that you have decided on the general tone of the spots. After that, write your copy, using no more than two major points in each sixty-second commercial, and one in each thirty-second one.

Then run each spot for a couple of weeks at a time. The last two weeks of the schedule, you might then rotate all of the spots, one after another, in your schedule. This way, all of your points will be made, but you will not confuse your listeners by trying to tell them too much in any one spot. In any case, since all the spots are related, you should probably try to see that all the spots have something in common. This is one place where your audio logo can be very helpful. If you don't have one, try to use a sound or some music behind each spot, letting that become a tie with all the others.

If you decide to produce commercials of this type, it is a good idea to let one station do the production and give you dubs to be run on any other station. That way, you will have the exact same spot on every station you use, which will also contribute to recognition. You may have to pay a production fee, but it will be worth it. (Stations normally do not charge for spots produced to be run on that station only; they do charge for dubs for other stations, and may well require studio and talent fees as well.)

How To Control The Session

If you are going to have someone produce a number of spots for you, try to be present when the recording session takes place. Go over the spot(s) with the announcer and with the engineer, paying attention to pronunciation of words, cues for sound effects, and the type of delivery you want. The delivery could be pushy and excited, or calm and inviting, or whatever. Then sit down and be quiet and let them produce the spot.

Listen to the playback. If there is a mistake, both the announcer and engineer may know it before you ever hear the playback. If there is a word or phrase you dislike, on the other hand, they will try to please you. But be careful. Don't bug them about each and every word. The people you are working with are professionals, and are as anxious as you are to turn out a good commercial. If they have suggestions about cutting or rearranging words or sentences, listen and decide if they are right.

Once you have given your approval to a *completed* spot, don't try to change it ten minutes later, because you thought of a better idea. Although the recording session is frequently a time for making corrections to copy, and honing a spot to its very finest point, it is not usually a good time to write new copy.

When you hear a spot read aloud with the appropriate music or sound effects, you will sometimes find that there are words or phrases which simply do not fit. This can be for reasons of timing, or because they make the commercial sound stiff. In such a case, even if it is your favorite phrase, you will be wise to listen to the announcer or engineer, at least until you have a considerable amount of experience in producing commercials.

A well-done spot should sound neither rushed nor draggy. It should move at a fair pace, and it should hold the interest from first word to last. Sound effects should be appropriate, not distracting, and musical backgrounds should suit the tone of the spot and not be so loud they drown out the announcer's voice.

If you must have the spot produced, and cannot attend the actual session, ask that you be given final approval. Most of the time, a spot can be played over the phone. If not, your rep (or someone else) can bring a cassette recording of the commercial to your office so that you may approve the final product. Again, be sure it is accurate, and be sure it conveys the image you were after when you wrote it.

Very seldom will a spot produced by professionals be completely off-base. If it is, ask that it be re-done, and be sure the announcer (or whoever is in charge of the session) is absolutely sure of what you want. It is better to do this with the original session, of course, but sometimes wires get crossed and there are misunderstandings.

Also, to prevent deadline problems, be sure you have the finished spot on tape well before your schedule will start. A week to ten days ahead is a good idea. If there are problems, you should have time to correct them. If you wait too late, you may discover that there is no studio time available for you to use. If you buy your schedule three to four weeks ahead, and plan to use that time to write and produce your spot, you shouldn't have any problems.

One of the nice things about radio is the fact that you can change both copy and schedules almost instantly (with a little luck). Suppose you are having a three-day sale on left-handed veeblefetzers. Suppose too that you sell out of them the first day of the sale, but manage to replace them with another product. You can write a new spot selling the new product, call the reps from the stations you are using, and get the new spot on the air within an hour or two. You may not be able to get a fully-produced spot, with music or sound effects, but you can get it on the air (and the dead spot off the air). For this reason, radio is an excellent medium for the small advertiser.

Making Schedule Changes

In the same way, most stations will cooperate if you need to add or delete spots from your schedule. Most contracts request two weeks' written notice of cancellation. In practice, many stations don't mind taking your schedule off the air if you run into a real problem of some sort. They don't like it, but they'll do it, so you should be very careful not to abuse this sort of thing with every schedule you buy. They will be better pleased if you can re-schedule the spots at a later time. They will also be happy to assist you if you need a schedule at sudden notice, provided that they have the spots to sell. If they do, you can buy them. But this is very poor planning on your part. You will have to take whatever you can get, and you may not be able to buy any spots at all at short notice. So don't fail to make a plan and stick to it as best you can.

Radio station reps are usually very helpful to new advertisers who need assistance with scheduling or copy. If you really have a problem, there are several ways to go. Check with your rep about the availability of a person at the station to assist you with copy. Ask about the possibility of hearing sample spots from other areas. If you still need help, see if one of your reps knows a free-lance copywriter who might be willing to assist you. And, of course, check with your manufacturers for the availability of radio scripts or tapes. You may not wish to use them exactly as they are, but they can be a big help in giving you ideas on which to build.

Radio is an excellent medium for the small advertiser, but like any other medium, use of radio must be planned with objectives in mind. These objectives are then scheduled according to a budget, and the copy must be the very best you can devise, in order to bring you the results you're looking for.

Chapter 8
Television In General

Many people consider television the strongest advertising medium available today. Most homes, except perhaps the poorest, have a television set. A large percentage of television sets are color. Therefore, an advertiser using TV can combine audio, video, color, movement, and graphics to create a message that will leave the viewer with a detailed impression of the products or services offered.

In addition, many advertisers have found that relaying a message to the audience member at a time when he/she is relaxed and comfortable at home (and supposedly receptive to such things) is an excellent time to make an impression.

Recently, with the advent of the video tape recorders, and other new methods, the viewer may see the message more than once.

The average television viewer sees several hours of TV a week. You would do well to check with your media rep for the latest figures on this, and of course, to find out just when who is watching what. If your town or city has more than one channel, be sure to search out the figures for all of them before you make any buys. To help you with this, here are some things you should know.

First, there is *network* programming, and *local* programming. Most television stations are affiliated with a national network, such as ABC, NBC, or CBS. These networks feed programs to local stations, which are then broadcast for pick-up by your television. (It is not at all necessary that you understand precisely how this is done.) In most cases, the station will air the program at the time it comes to them. In some cases, they will record the program for a later air time.

The station also has other program sources. Programs produced at the station itself, such as local news, perhaps an interview show, perhaps a kiddie show, can be aired in addition to or in place of a network program. Another source is the kind of service which allows the station to purchase an outdated series for airing—anything from old movies to personality shows.

If you check with your reps, you will probably find that your local stations run a combination of network and locally-produced shows. The local programs are generally aimed at producing a feeling of immediacy and (perhaps) community involvement.

The network shows allow the local station time for commercial breaks before and after. In a long show, there are usually one or two "station breaks" where a station can run in a local commercial. In a local program, the station can run commercials within the program, as well as at the beginning and end.

Getting Ideas

Before you try to consider television, spend a couple of evenings in front of your set. A good time is from 6 p.m. to midnight. Jot down which are the local and which are the network shows. Then check out other times of the day—early morning, midday, early evening, and after midnight. It's also a good idea to see what the stations are presenting on weekends. Use the listings in your daily paper if such things are available, or have each station send you a copy of its day-by-day schedule. Consider the probable audience for each show. Then, call your reps, and ask for the survey figures for the various shows.

Try to be sure each station uses the same survey so that you obtain a realistic comparison. When you have the audience figures, broken down as far as possible into groupings by age and sex, compare the figures with your own customer profile/target audience.

A typical television day looks something like this:

Morning: From 6 a.m. to 9 a.m. The programming is likely to be aimed at a general audience—perhaps news, weather, sports, a national interview show, a local interview show.

Midday: This time is usually reserved for game shows, on-going stories (soaps), perhaps a mid-morning movie. It is aimed primarily at housewives.

Early Fringe: From about 4 p.m. til 7:30 p.m., the programming varies. You may find kiddie shows, news, or comedy shows scheduled during these hours. Many stations run at least one news show during this time period, and most of these are locally-produced. Some networks offer a half-hour of news by a nationally-known person, which the station will run adjacent to its own news show.

Prime Time: From about 7:30 p.m. or 8 p.m. til 11 p.m. is the prime time for television. It is during this time that the networks make the biggest efforts to schedule programs which will attract and hold the largest possible viewing audience. Competition is fierce, the audience figures are usually high, and prices for commercials are the highest.

11 p.m. to CC: From 11 p.m. until the station signs off (if it does), the audience begins to dwindle. People head for bed, and programming changes to appeal to those who might be awake. Some stations run a news show directly after the last prime time show, then go to a network show featuring a well-known personality, or to a movie, or even to an all-night discussion of local or national news.

Television differs from radio in this respect: radio is usually scheduled in blocks of time, as we have seen. On the other hand, in spite of the divisions as we have just discussed, television is scheduled in smaller blocks. Normally these blocks are from one-half hour to an hour, sometimes (as with a special or a long movie) from two to three hours. Each separate program, particularly during prime time, can have a different audience rating and commercials can vary in cost. A spot which costs you $100 at 6:30 p.m. can cost you $1,000 at 9 p.m.

Due to these differences, you must be very careful when you budget for television. Keep in mind that you are aiming at your specific target audience, and look at the ratings again. Your should be able to find several programs which reach a large percentage of the people you're looking for, without costing your entire weekly budget. If you buy several of these less-costly shows, you will gain an excellent "reach" as well as a desirable "frequency."

For instance, the local 6 p.m. news may provide you with 40% to 50% of the viewing audience who you would get if you bought a spot at 9 p.m. If the local news spot costs you a fourth of the prime time spot, you can buy four spots, thus reaching a large percentage of the people, and reaching some of them as many as two or three times.

Be sure to work with your reps on this. They are aware of where your audience is, and they should be willing to help you get the most audience for the amount of money you spend. Try giving them a budget to work with, a time frame, and an idea of what you want to accomplish with your television advertising. Let them come up with suggestions. Remember to keep all your personal dislikes and likes out of the discussion. If everyone over the age of twenty-one is watching a silly show called "The Man from Jupiter," and the show has horrible beasts and worse special effects, you probably think it should be sent to Jupiter on the first available flight. But remember that everyone over twenty-one is going to see your spot, and if the spot is good, they will remember it. That's what you're after. Your opinions don't matter—the facts and figures do.

Budgeting

Budgeting for television can be tricky. You may (or may not) be aware that a national advertiser, buying a network spot, can pay as much for one spot as you would spend on all your advertising in two years. The costs are enormous. However, on a local basis, spots can cost anywhere from $10 to $1000, depending on where and when they are scheduled. Sometimes, a particular spot may cost more, or the range may differ due to your particular market. Generally speaking, television can cost either a little or a lot, depending on where you place the spots. Let's look at some specific times.

Morning

The audience in this time period can range from the business person catching a glimpse of the news, to the homemaker having coffee, to the preschooler who has nothing better to do. It is not necessarily the largest audience of the TV day, and it is for the most part extremely varied. Spots during this time are generally not expensive, and can be effective as part of your schedule. This depends on your target audience. Look carefully at the ratings for these times for all the television stations in your area. If you find that one or two stations have a fair number of viewers within your target grouping, consider buying there. If, on the other hand, you want to reach only a small group of people and none of them are registered in the surveys, you may want to stay out of this time on television.

Using the formula you learned for CPM in the chapter on radio, figure the efficiency of the money you propose to spend in this time period on television. If it looks good, fine. But if, when you compare it to other time periods, it shows an exorbitant CPM with little reach, you may be wise to concentrate on other areas.

Midday

The audience during this time can be more specifically pinpointed. Consider the facts of life in your city. If the majority of the people between the ages of 25 and 49 leave home and work from nine in the morning til five in the afternoon, the midday audience must be made up of those people who do not work. They do not work for reasons of age, or for desire. On the other hand, if the population in your city is composed of shift workers in several large factories and plants, the midday audience is quite likely to include a larger variety of people. Again, do your homework here. Lots of advertisers for many years have considered the hours from ten a.m. til four p.m. the ideal time to sell soap powder, cleaning agents, food items, and so forth to the "housewife."

You should be aware that this idea is changing. More and more women are joining the work force and leaving home. Many women, who were formerly totally dependent on their husbands for money are now working either part-or full-time, thus giving you two points to consider. One, that woman you're selling to may not be there to get your message, and two, she may be out spending her own money on things she wants and needs, as well as items for her family or home. Try to take extra care in finding out who is watching television during these hours, apply your CPM and your research about your target audience. If the time looks good for your business, add it to your schedule. It will probably cost you a little more than the early morning time, and less than the fringe or prime time.

Fringe

This is an interesting time of day for two reasons. One, the programming can be aimed at "family" or "kids" or "adults." Many stations run lighter programs during the hours from four to six, in an effort to attract both the kids and the adults who may be home from work. From six p.m. til maybe seven or seven-thirty, things are likely to be a little more serious. The stations will program local or national news shows, as well as special features.

The second reason for interest is the fact that costs may be far below those during prime time (though higher than midday), and in many cases the audience figures are almost as high as they are during prime times. These facts make for an excellent CPM, as well as offering you excellent reach and frequency. Do some very careful evaluation of the fringe times in your area, before you let a rep convince you to buy only prime time. If your budget is limited, the fringe can allow you to buy the TV exposure you need, without sacrificing the frequency.

Prime

Well, here it is. The time of day when most people watch the most television, and the advertiser pays the most money to reach those people. This is the time during which the networks try to schedule the best programs they have in order to build the biggest audiences. They can then charge enormous amounts of money for commercials. Fine. Look at the prime time programming in your area. Consider the audience figures carefully. Let your rep help you with decisions about whether your spot would do a better job placed before a popular program, or between it and another program. If your research shows that one spot a week adjacent to a specific program will do you more good at a reasonable cost per thousand than two or three spots at other times, then if your budget allows it, buy it, by all means. Again, don't allow yourself to be oversold by the popularity of a program if the viewers are all fifty years of age and you're selling to a target audience of twenty-year-olds.

11 p.m. to CC

Spots during this time usually cost less than prime time or early fringe times. They cost slightly more than morning or midday times. The audience usually drops considerably from prime time figures, but may include just the specific people you need to reach. Use of spots here, in combination with other times, can be of use to some advertisers, depending on the available audience within the marketing area, and their viewing habits. As always, check the CPM, the make-up of the audience in relation to your target, and your budget.

Something else for you to consider is special programming. The networks will occasionally schedule a big sports event, a beauty pageant, a speech by the President, a variety show starring a popular artist. Spots adjacent to this type of show are sometimes offered at a premium rate, or sometimes are a special rate if you buy a "package" which includes other times on the station. Your rep should always call you if such times or programs become available. He should try to give you at least an educated estimate of the probable audience as well as explain why this special program will be of assistance to you. Don't dismiss him out of hand. Some of these shows might be just what you need to make your business viable. Don't blow your budget on them, but do take them into consideration in your planning.

Check with your rep for a list of specials planned by the networks. They will usually have one, including the times and dates the network proposes to air the shows. This may all change, but at least you won't be caught totally by surprise by them. For instance, if you see on the list a show that is sure to appeal to the whole family, you might check with your rep and be sure he knows to call you when the time and date are confirmed, and when he has prices for spots available to discuss.

Rates for television spots vary, of course, in different markets, on different stations, within a single market. They also vary during different time periods of the day or week on single stations. Generally, television stations have the same type of "grid card" we discussed in the chapter about radio. There is a little less switching from grid to grid within a short time span.

Seasons in TV Programming

Television also has "seasons." The fall season, when the new network programming appears, and children have gone back to school, and people are beginning to think about the holiday season ahead, is generally the best time for the station. They are busier then than at any other time. The programming is the best it is all year, and an advertiser can be sold spots at a higher price. After the holiday season, and after the new programs have failed or lost their newness, advertising normally slows down a bit. Then stations can sell spots for less. This is true of regular programming. A "special" with a star or two in it, a very important sports event, or some other special programming, can still command a high price.

Still later in the year, when most of the programs are starting into reruns, when the weather breaks, and the kids are out of school, there may be still another rate break for the advertiser. Again, we are not talking about summer sports specials, or the occasional special for the kids, but normal week-to-week programming by the station and the network.

Toward the end of the summer, things begin to pick up again, as advertisers aim messages at school-age children. Advertisers aim for their parents, at college-bound men and women, at homemakers and working couples to get things in shape for fall and winter. There are previews of new programs, and very quickly, the new shows themselves. By the time we are well into fall, the television networks and stations are all geared up and rolling into their prime selling season. This cycle is not necessarily the same in each city or metro market, but if you stay in touch with your reps, you will probably find that there are times when you can buy prime time spots at less cost than usual. If these low prices for television can be worked into your own selling plans, you can use television to great advantage.

For instance, if you sell either above-ground or in-ground swimming pools, you may discover that prices for TV spots during (say) May, June, and July are far below prices for the same shows during September, October, and November. If you have planned your yearly budget correctly, you will know about such price advantages and be able to use them to achieve your advertising goals.

Pricing Criteria

Television stations tend to price spots on three grids. The prime rate is the top price for a show. It means that your spot will run exactly where you want it to run, on the day you prefer, and that no one can bump you out. The second rate can be preempted by an advertiser paying the top rate, but normally requires that the station give you notice of perhaps two weeks. This enables you to agree to pay the top rate if the placement of your spot is vital to a particular goal. The third rate is comparable to the ROS rate on radio. It allows you to purchase spots inexpensively, but gives you no guarantee that your spot will run on the day you planned for it to air. Either one of the other two prices will cause your spot to be preempted and moved to another day, though not to another program.

These three grids are normally available during the year, and depending on how busy the station is at any given time, you may pay any of the prices, or a combination of prices, depending on how sold-out they are in the time periods you want to use.

As an example, suppose you want to buy an Early News spot. The grid prices may be something like $150, $200, and $250 for a thirty-second commercial. If the station is not busy, and there is no huge demand for these spots by other advertisers, you may be able to buy your spot at $150 and have it run exactly where you want it. If, on the other hand, the spots in that time are staying close to sold-out, you may have to pay the top price to be sure the spot will air on the day you need it.

TV stations also offer packages from time to time. These usually involve the purchase of several specific spots (as, for instance, in a series of sports events), plus a number of other time periods ranging throughout the broadcast day. The packages normally last for thirteen weeks, or the length of the scheduled sports events. You may use your other spots anywhere within that time. There is usually a price break. If you have planned ahead, and the package will be a good addition to your advertising, it can be an excellent buy. Be sure to establish a relationship with your reps that ensures you are informed as soon as possible when any such package becomes available.

Television is also subject to price increases from time to time. There is usually some rate protection for you if you have bought a schedule for a minimum of thirteen or twenty-six weeks. That is, if you have bought two spots a week in the news at $200 per spot, and the rate goes to $250, you can probably continue to pay the lower rate for thirty or sixty or ninety days, depending on the station's policy. This is another reason why it is wise to buy ahead when you can.

Scheduling

As with all advertising, the secret to making television work for you at efficient dollar costs and results obtained is to plan ahead.

If you know in January or February that you will need a heavy ad campaign to start your summer selling season in May or June, sit down and figure out what you will need in the various media. Plan your budgets, and call in your reps. They will be glad to help with specific planning, but there are a couple of things you should know that will help you out.

First, television requires frequency, as does radio. This means that if you are planning a one-week sale, the five days prior to the sale and the sale days will be your heavy advertising period. If you need advertising to carry you through a season, on the other hand, you'll need a longer schedule with fewer spots per week.

There is another interesting phenomenon about TV advertising. If you advertise fairly heavily for say, two weeks, and establish yourself with the viewing audience, you can then NOT advertise. Perhaps you can advertise very lightly for a week to ten days, and then come back with a schedule of perhaps two-thirds the strength of the initial plan. The audience will be convinced that you are on the air heavily all the time. This kind of "run–skip–run" schedule works very well for the small advertiser who can't afford to stay on the air heavily all the time. It saves money without damaging reach and frequency.

Be sure to talk with your reps about this kind of possibility in your market area. You may find that after an initial week or two you can skip the next week, run lightly the following week, and come in a little more heavily still later, thus stretching your television budget as far as possible.

Also, check for very popular time periods. Examine the possibility of running one spot on each station during the same time. To use the news as an example again, see what the audience ratings are during the 6 p.m. to 7 p.m. time slot on the stations in your market. If they are close in numbers on two or three stations, try running one spot on each station during that time. If the numbers are right, you will hit a large portion, sometimes almost all, of the viewing audience in your area. If you can repeat this kind of schedule every two or three days for ten days to two weeks, using at least two or three good time periods (maybe early news, late news, and the break at 7:30 p.m.), you will convince a large number of people that you are on the air all the time. Your reach and frequency should be excellent, and your CPM reasonable.

All this is necessarily a little nebulous, since each market will differ. Your area may have more or fewer TV stations. The programming may be entirely different. Maybe the stations all schedule an hour of news at 11 p.m., and none at 6 p.m. But if you will work with your reps, you should be able to come up with some sort of a pattern that will allow you to reach as many people as possible at a reasonable cost.

Differences Between TV & Radio Buys

Buying television is different from buying radio. The two mediums are different in structure. Be sure to take the time to familiarize yourself with both of them before you decide for or against using either one. You will hear that TV is "too expensive" for the small advertiser. You needn't let other people make your decisions for you. Look at the audiences, see how well you can pinpoint your target audience, check your cost per thousand, and see whether in some cases television may be your most efficient buy, regardless of the cost per spot.

Trends in Cable TV and Recorders

You should also be aware of the trends in your areas regarding cable TV, and television tape recorders and disc recorders. These are all fairly new in most areas, however, they are gaining in popularity.

Cable provides a wide choice of channels, some of which offer full-length, first-run movies with no commercials. This may or may not cut into the available viewing audience for your local commercial channels. The recorders and disc players may have another effect. Since most of them now permit the viewer to eliminate commercials if so desired, your message may be edited out. On the other hand, in some cases a person may see a spot several times if a particular program is recorded and played over and over again. Try to keep in close touch with these different television systems, so that you know how much they are likely to affect the viewing audience in your market. At some point, the national surveys will probably take all of this into account. They may state something so simple as noting that although there are 300,000 homes with TV's in a certain area, the actual available audience for commercial TV may be only half that. A good television rep will also be able to help you keep up with this sort of data, and should be willing to show you where and when you can run your spots to the best advantage on the commercial channels.

Chapter 9
The Television Commercial

Once you have decided that you would like to run some television, you are immediately faced with the problem of creating a commercial. It is not something you will be able to do alone. You will need the assistance of a production studio, whether it is an independent one, or whether you use the facilities at one of the stations in your town. In order for you to be able to use television effectively, you should know a little about how to produce a spot, in order that you can contribute ideas which will work.

First, let's look at the different media available for your use:

1. **Film:** A television spot can be made on 16mm film, just as you would make a movie, including sound.

2. **Videotape:** You can make a spot directly on 2″ videotape, much as you would record an audio spot on ¼″ audio tape. The result is usually very clear, and very smooth, but tends to lack the softness of film.

3. **Slides & Audio:** You can use color slides, plus an audio tape, and create a spot which is put on videotape for airing.

4. **Graphics/Pictures/Audio:** You may use any combination of visual images, plus your audio, to create the commercial.

In most cases, television stations use the 2″ high-band tape for airing, so no matter how the spot originates, it will probably be transferred to videotape at some point.

You should also be aware of the tremendous variety of ways you can go about producing a spot. For instance, you can have an announcer stand in the studio in front of the camera and read your copy. The announcer may or may not be provided with a background, such as a slide showing your place of business. This is the simplest use of TV. You can choose six or seven slides, have them appear on the screen one after another, with an announcer talking over them, though he/she does not appear. You may hire a cameraman and a director and talent, and have the talent (announcer) visit your place of business. While there, he will discuss what you have to sell, while the cameraman is filming him on location. You may do the same sort of thing with a videotape crew. You may set up an elaborate scene in a studio, and have one or more people on camera. There is an enormous variety of techniques available to you, but before you can make use of any of them, you must go through much the same process you did when you created your radio spot.

Perhaps the easiest way to start is to make your list again. Decide what you want the spot to say, and the general tone you want it to have. List the facts to be included. Keep in mind at all times that you will be able to use both video and audio images to convey your meanings. Once you have all this well in hand, make up a storyboard.

The Storyboard

A storyboard is a simple technique for putting information down on paper, so that you and the people you will be working with during the actual creation of the spot will understand what you want. The audio and visual components of your commercial will be apparent.

Normally, a thirty-second television commercial will allow you approximately six to eight visual changes, and perhaps sixty words of copy. Following is a blank storyboard. It is easy to make one for your own use, by drawing the appropriate lines on a sheet of blank typing paper.

Figure 31.
Sample of television commercial storyboard.

Video I: *(Description* *or* *Sketch of Visual)* *number of seconds.*	Video II:	
Audio I:	**Audio II:**	

This kind of plan will help you see just where your audio and visual components will fall, and will make an actual production session much easier on all concerned.

Another method, which may be used separately or in conjunction with the storyboard, is the following:

Figure 32.
Video and audio instructions for TV spot.

VIDEO	AUDIO
Open: Logo camera card, full screen, hold 3 seconds,	The Store is having a super swing into spring sale...
dissolve to Slide #1 cut to slide #2 cut to slide #3	The entire stock of women's clothing at The Store
Cut to Camera Card #2, "SAVE 30% to 60%"	has been reduced 30 to 60 percent...for this week only.
Cut to Slide #4	New spring dresses, suits,
Cut to Slide #5	bathing suits, and playclothes are all on sale at big, big savings.
Dissolve to Logo card Reveal 1st address, same card Reveal 2nd address, same card	Swing into spring at The Store, on Park Avenue and on West Main.

As you can see, writing a TV spot is more complex than writing for radio. You must at all times plan on both audio and video. This will not be easy for you the first time or two you do it, so be sure to work closely with the people who will actually help you produce the spot. Your TV rep can be very helpful, and will probably be more than willing to put you in touch with the creative staff at his/her station. However, in order for you to make the best use of the help they can give you, you must have some idea of what you want.

Let's assume you want to create an image spot for your business. This spot will be used over and over again for a long period of time. First, decide exactly what you are trying to convey. Then, picture in your mind some visuals that will help, while trying to decide on appropriate copy lines.

Do you want to show the outside of your store? The inside? Do you want to use a testimonial from a pleased customer? Do you want a very sincere announcer pointing out some of the advantages of using your service? All of this can be discussed with the creative staff with whom you will be working, and they can probably offer excellent suggestions.

This initial stage is also the time to consider the cost of the production. Charges will be made for studio time, tape or film, location filming, art or camera cards, slides—in fact, for everything that goes into the final production of the commercial. Don't be afraid to ask what things cost. If one way of doing your commercial looks much too expensive, tell them it won't do, and try again. Television production costs can range from inexpensive to very expensive, so be sure you know what you are letting yourself in for.

Since the commercial we are discussing now is an image spot, to be used for a long period of time, you should know about one other thing. This is the "video logo."

The Video Logo

A video logo can be very important if you will be using television on a consistent basis. It is a way of tying all your television spots to one another, so that your business becomes easily recognizable.

Remember the logo symbol or type style you are using on all your printed materials? Bring it out and dust it off, for here is where you use it again.

A video logo is usually visual only, and is five to eight seconds in length. Look at your logo. How can you make it exciting and attention-getting for a television viewer? Here are some suggestions. Think about them, and then discuss them with the production staff, who may have other ideas to add to these.

1. Movement. A word or logo on a television screen can appear to move. It requires the use of "edits," and some technical skill on the part of the producer, but can be very effective. Picture your logo very tiny, in the top right corner of the screen. From there, it goes to the middle of the top of the screen, and grows slightly larger. Then it moves to the middle left of the screen, still growing, then to the actual center of the screen to full size. This is several separate moves and stops, which will appear to the viewer as one continuous move on the finished tape.

2. Reveal. Your logo/name can appear on the screen letter-by-letter, as though someone were writing it out in front of the viewer.

3. Flashing. The entire logo/name can flash on and off several times.

4. Color Changes. Each letter of your name can be a different color, or the entire name can change from color to color.

These are simple suggestions, making use of the color and movement available on television. There are many other ways of creating visual interest, so be sure to ask for suggestions. Also, keep your eyes open and watch national commercials for ideas.

Once you have decided on a basic video logo, you may want to combine it with the music or sound effect you have chosen for your audio logo. In this way, you can keep your identity in all the media. Your newspaper print logo will appear on television, and your audio logo from your radio spots will tie in. If you do this, you will find that you become more identifiable faster than if you keep these media totally separate from each other.

Now that you have your ideas firmly in mind, you will go into the studio and create your own "donut" for use in all your television commercials. That is, you will have an open and a close on tape. These can then be used with any copy you desire at any time, and all your spots will have a close relationship with one another. The image spot we have been planning will start with your open. You will then fill in the middle with the copy for your image spot, and the spot will end with your close. When you are ready to do another commercial, you can come back to the logo tape and re-use the open and close, again filling the donut with the appropriate audio and video.

The open and close can be used together for each spot, or you may use just the open or just the close if you need more time for body copy in a particular commercial. The creating of this special logo open and close will allow you more leeway in planning other spots. It will also give your commercials a far more professional look than if you simply flash a slide of your storefront on the screen.

Once you have the logo tape ready, you can use the donut for a special event or sale, combining it with visuals. These visuals would be camera cards, slides, or video tapes of products and prices, with an announcer's voice. The staff at the production studio will be able to offer suggestions, whether you're working with a TV station or with an independent production house.

Keep in mind that many manufacturers will have slides or film, and sometimes videotape, that you can use and adapt to your particular needs. This material, when combined with your own logo, can give your spots a very nice, professional look. This is especially true if you use your audio logo and a good announcer.

If you haven't any materials available, you can bring samples into the studio and tape them there, if your product lends itself to this technique. Or you may bring the tape or film crew to any location you choose and create your own footage to be used for a specific commercial. If you do this, try to get some extra shots of different areas of your store, or different views of what you sell. These can be used later in other spots. Such extra shots are generally called "wild footage."

Before you decide precisely what you want to do, do be sure to check on the costs. You wouldn't want to be very unpleasantly surprised to find that your TV production has eaten up your budget for two or three months. If you have to make your commercials inexpensively in order to run a schedule, fine. But be sure the spots are interesting, that they move quickly but are not rushed, that they are coordinated with your radio, newspaper, or other media, and that they convey a desirable image of your store or services to your target audience. Be careful not to offend. If you wish to use a humorous approach, be sure the commercial really is funny and also in good taste. Don't bore the viewer and don't try to crowd too many things into any one spot.

If you can be present during a television production session, this will be good experience for you. Watch to be sure your wishes are carried out, and, of course, be very sure that the final product has your complete approval. Please refrain from trying to take over and run the session. That's best left to the professional.

If you have a question, by all means ask it when the announcer is finished. In the making of any TV spot, there are little breaks where you will feel comfortable about asking your questions. When you have suggestions, try to make them at an opportune moment. On the other hand, don't be afraid to speak up if there is something going on that you particularly dislike.

If you cannot be present while the spot is being made, insist on viewing it before it goes on the air. Again, as you did for the radio commercial, be sure that the important information is clearly presented and that everything (either audio or video) is correct and accurate. Correct your mistakes before you go on the air.

Television can be an excellent advertising medium for the small advertiser. It is important to be sure that the schedule is carefully planned with goals and with the target audience in mind. It is also important that your commercials be produced in a professional manner. You may have to rely heavily on the rep from your local television station, and on the creative staff, until you learn your way around. But don't let that stop you from considering TV in your planning. Use it when your budget and goals indicate it will be efficient, and in conjunction with your other advertising. You may find it is just what you needed to accomplish your purpose.

If you need ideas on how others in your business have successfully used television, check to find out if a local station is a member of the Television Advertising Bureau. As in radio, video tapes of successful spots are available for viewing. Ask to see a tape on your business or products, or a tape of the top 25 or 50 spots of the year. One station in your city is likely to have such a service available, so make use of it if you need to see examples before creating your own commercials.

If you're looking at such a tape, be sure to have a pencil and pad handy to jot down any idea that particularly strikes you. You don't necessarily want to copy any of the spots exactly; you may wish to use an idea for a visual from one, copy points from another, musical ideas from a third. Make a note of anything that interests you, and of any technique you may not understand. Ask about it. Find out what the capabilities of the station and production staff are; check on prices to produce a commercial similar to one you like on the tape. Some may be too expensive, but chances are you'll come up with several ideas for spots or campaigns that will be well within your budget. A production person may be able to translate an idea into something less expensive, but no less effective.

A good TV spot will bring you the traffic you need; a bad one won't. However, a commercial that you think is downright horrid may be highly effective in accomplishing its purpose, while a slicker, prettier spot may leave the public cold. So don't condemn any spot out of hand; look at it from all angles, to see if it can work to accomplish your personal goals. If it can, then use it.

Chapter 10
Magazines, Billboards, Bus Cards, Direct Mail

I've lumped these four media together in one place since (in some ways) they are related to one another. First, though they are major media, they are not necessarily the first media to be considered by the small advertiser. Second, they all require use of the eyes only for the reception of the advertising message.

Magazines are print, as is direct mail. Billboards and bus cards are more properly considered "outdoor" advertising. They can all have a place in the ad budget of the small business, but generally speaking, they should be used as *additions* to your budget, rather than the basis around which you plan the major portion of your advertising. Before we discuss the "how's," let's take a brief look at the "why's"—that is, what each of these media can do for you.

Magazines

First, when I speak of magazines I am primarily concerned with local magazines. There is perhaps a city magazine covering your immediate area, or even a county or regional magazine which lists subscribers in two or three locations close enough to you to provide some reach to your target audience. There are also regional editions of some of the major magazines. If your budget allows expenditure for the regional editions, you may certainly find them of value. However, for our purposes here, I will be referring only to the local, or city, magazine.

These publications can be put out by independent publishers, or by the Chamber of Commerce, or other groups. Normally, they contain editorial matter of interest to citizens in the immediate area. Sometimes they will offer a combination of news articles of different types, including "shorts" and feature-length, in-depth stories; reviews of movies, local plays, or musical events; a section on restaurants with comments on quality as well as a simple listing; perhaps a poem or two, or a short story; a section on recipes or housekeeping. The variety of contents depends on the town and on the tastes of the readers. These magazines normally try to sell ads to local advertisers, and such ads may well be a good buy. This depends on what you are selling, and the goals you expect to reach.

Subscribers

Before you decide for or against using such a magazine, find out who is subscribing to it. If the magazine has been around for a year or more, some sort of audience survey has probably been taken. You need to know how many *paid* subscribers the magazine boasts. "Pass-alongs"* are not to be relied upon. If possible, check zip codes or addresses, thus obtaining some idea of where the subscribers live in relation to your store or business. Check on average ages, on sex, and on household income if this is possible. If you sell a product aimed at children, or parents of children, check on family make-up. If the magazine hasn't done some sort of survey and has been in business for a year or two, they are slipping up.

If the magazine can offer specific information on their readership, it has a much better chance of convincing you (as the advertiser) that an ad placed here is a good investment. You will have a better idea of how likely your ad is to reach your target audience, as well.

If such a magazine exists in your city, and you are considering using it, ask for the information you need before you buy. Most of the time, the salesperson who calls on you will provide you with the facts at the same time you are presented with the rate card and mechanical requirements. If the salesperson doesn't do this, and if the information you need is not available, you may do well to consider other methods of reaching your target audience.

Direct Mail

This is just as it sounds. In fact, you probably receive direct mail advertising both at home and at your place of business. All advertising

---

*Pass-along readership consists of people who read the magazine by borrowing it from a friend, reading it in a waiting room, or reading it in the library, but who do not subscribe. There is virtually no accurate way to determine pass-along readership.

has as its purpose the giving of information and the creation of the incentive to buy. Any advertising is to tell what is for sale, why the reader needs it, and to convince him that he can no longer do without the product or service, and why he should order it without further delay.

A direct mail piece also does one other thing besides the above. It attempts to convince the recipient to buy NOW, and puts the order blank right in his hand. Direct mail certainly works. It can work for you, too. But you must be careful to design your direct mail carefully, and use it to achieve specific goals, if it is to be an efficient use of your advertising dollars.

Billboards and Bus Cards

These can also have a place in your budget, but there are some things you need to remember if your budget is a small one. First, newspaper and magazine ads, and even direct mail, allow the audience unlimited time in which to read and absorb your advertising message. Radio and television spots allow a minimum of ten seconds (usually thirty or sixty seconds) and either audio and/or video images to enhance the message. Billboards and bus cards, on the other hand, must be read and absorbed in two to five seconds if the reader is traveling in a moving vehicle. Five seconds is not very much time in which to convey an important message about your product or service. Also, the boards or cards are competing with traffic for the driver's attention, and with conversation in the car as well as (perhaps) the radio or other distractions.

It is very important, therefore, that you plan your billboards very carefully. They can be an excellent addition to your normal advertising, if you can afford them. If you can afford only one, you may find one board near your place of business, and use it to give directions. If you are having a special sale for one month, you may be able to buy either billboards or bus cards for that brief period, and find that they are well within your budget.

Magazine Advertising

If you are planning to use magazine ads, either in the local magazine for your city, or in some of the regional editions of nationally-known magazines, the first thing you should do is to sit down with a magazine in your hand. Preferably, this should be the one you are planning to use. Look at it closely. Avoid the tendency to skim. Here are some things to notice.

First, the inside cover, the inside back cover, and outside back cover are preferred positions. They are normally in color, and are usually the most expensive ads you can buy. Just as expensive is a "double-truck" (two-page spread) in the middle of the magazine. These are sold as full-page ads, and they can certainly command a great deal of attention if they are well done.

Glance at the magazine you intend to use, and note the ads in these positions. If they are advertisements for local companies and stores, you may well find that they are fairly large businesses or well-known.

Second, look at the first page. This is the first page inside on the right hand facing the cover. This is also a preferred position, if the magazine sells ad space here.

Third, flip to the middle of the book. See if there is a double-truck ad. This can also be a very impressive position, and can be in color or black and white. Two pages opposite each other provide a great deal of room for you to use illustrations, or photographs, or to discuss a number of different items or ideas. Again, you may pay a premium for this position.

Now, go through the rest of the magazine, with the rate card in hand. Look carefully at the sizes and shapes of the advertisements. They may vary from magazine to magazine, but you will probably find a breakdown like this:

Full page
½ page vertical/½ page horizontal
⅓ page vertical/⅓ page horizontal
⅔ page
¼ page
1/6 page
1/12 page

Some magazines will not offer the smallest two sizes. Some may not offer the vertical/horizontal choices. But most of them will offer some variation of these sizes.

Look at all the ads carefully, noting which size seems to attract and hold your attention. For instance, you may find that the ⅓ page vertical offers more striking possibilities than the ⅓ page horizontal, which may appear square and dull.

Figure 33. Sizes and shapes of magazine ads.

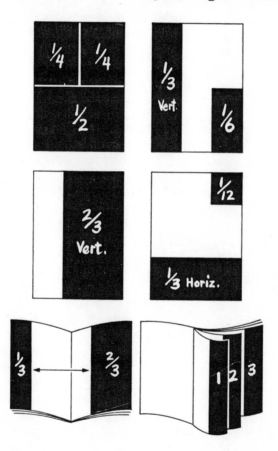

   Take note of the position on the page. The outside right of the right hand page is usually considered the best position. The top is preferred over the bottom of the page. Decide whether you prefer a border, or whether you like ad copy which seems to "float" in white space. Note the fact that some full-page ads spread all the way to the edge of the page, and some are surrounded by borders or simply stop at the same point on the page as the editorial matter. (That is, they have around them the same border of white which you find on editorial pages.)

You should be aware of all of these things when planning your own magazine ads. Once you feel fairly familiar with them, look at your rate card. You will probably find that a full-page is fairly expensive, so you may want to consider one of the other sizes. A ¼-page, ⅓-page, or ½-page advertisement can be just as attention-getting as a full page, if it is correctly designed.

Discounts

While you are looking at the rate card, note the discounts for long-term contracts. Most magazines offer reduced rates for longer schedules. For instance, glance at this fictitious rate card:

Figure 34. Sample rate card.

AD SIZE	1X	3X	6X	12X
full page	$750	$675	$625	$600
½ page	$600	$550	$500	$475
⅓ page	$400	$375	$345	$310

Assuming that the magazine comes out twelve times (12X) a year, you can save money by planning ahead. What these rates mean is that you can contract to place an ad three, six, or twelve times within a calendar year from the first insertion. In most cases, the ads do not have to be consecutive. You do not have to run January, February, and March, one after the other. You may wish to run in January, September, and December, and you will have satisfied the 3X rate requirement. If you can plan in advance this way, you will save money, although in some cases, if you run six times without a contract, the magazine will still give you the six-time rate. They charge you less for the last ad you run. However, if you contract to run six times, and only run three, you will probably be "short-rated." That is, you will receive a bill at the end of the calendar year charging you for the balance due on the 3X rate.

Using the above prices, this would mean:

Contract for 6X (to run ⅓ page ads)
6 × $345 = a bill to you for $345 for each ad you run, normally sent monthly. If you run only three ads, you should have paid $375 per ad, so you will be billed $30 × 3 = $90.00 "short-rate."

On the other hand, if you contract for three ads and actually run six, the last ad you run will probably be billed at the 6X rate, less the difference in price for each of the ads you have run before, or 5 × the $30 price difference = $150. Your last ad should cost you $345 - $150 = $295.

Most local magazines will work with you on this type of thing. If you are planning to use the national magazines, do be sure you fully understand their rate structures and contracts so you don't end up paying more than you need.

Looking further at the rate card, you may notice some other kinds of charges. Color is extra. Sometimes you can use black plus one color for a nominal extra fee, but a full-color ad will cost considerably more than a black-and-white ad. Also, color is usually available only on certain sized ads. If you send in completely "camera-ready" artwork, you probably won't be charged anything for production. But if you give the magazine's production department a layout and some art, and they have to typeset the ad, you will be charged for this service. For this reason, you are probably just as well off to let your own artist do your mechanical. That way, you will have full control of your ad, and can be sure it will be exactly as you want it.

Deadlines

Another thing to notice about magazine advertising is deadlines. Most magazines require space reservations about two months in advance of publication date. They require finished ad copy or mechanicals at least a month ahead of publication. This means you have to plan in advance.

If you are going to insert an ad in the December issue, buy your space by the first of October and try to have the finished art to the magazine by October 25th or so. Check with the rep for the magazine you plan to use for specific deadlines, since they may differ. If you are planning on running an ad every other month, you will have to be aware of deadlines all through the year. In a case like this, it's a good idea to mark your calendar with the deadline dates, and then with the date one month ahead of each deadline. Then you will have plenty of time to work with your artist on new ads.

Besides the single insertion per issue, which we have just be discussing, there are other ways to use magazine advertisements. For instance, you can buy three ⅓-page vertical ads, and pay a premium to be sure they are inserted on the right hand page, right side, on three consecutive pages (one on page 9, one on 11, and one on 13). Or, you could buy a ⅓-page ad to be inserted on the left-hand page, left side, and a ⅔-page ad to be inserted on the right-hand facing page, outside right columns, and continue your message from the left-hand ad to the right-hand ad. Special positioning such as this may cost you a bit more than a straight ad, but it offers a way to give your ads some variety.

Special Deals

Some magazines will from time to time offer "special sections." These may be anything from a guide for newcomers to the city, to special real estate sections, to home furnishings, to fashion. Depending on the subject matter, such specials may have a life far beyond that of the normal once-a-month issue. They may even be offered for sale separately.

If such a section becomes available in the magazine you are planning to use, look at it from the point of view of continuing to reach the target audience. If you were trying to reach young married couples between the ages of twenty-five and thirty-five, and the magazine has a fair number of subscribers in this bracket, you would still need to consider very carefully, especially if the special section happens to be discussing care for the aged. These special sections usually cost a bit more than the normal ads, and in the above case, you may or may not feel that this type of section would reach those people who make up your target audience better than the regular magazine does. As with all advertising, don't buy on impulse, or because the rep happens to be particularly persuasive one day.

Once you have decided on the size of the ad you wish to run, you have the same situation we discussed in the chapter on newspapers. You've bought yourself some space, and now you must fill it. You can use the same guidelines we have discussed before, keeping in mind that you are out to get results, not to win the prize for the prettiest ad on the block.

Creating the Ad

Let's glance at some more ideas that may help with creating your ads, and with writing copy. Remember that in the first chapter we discussed the fact that you must know *what* you are selling *to whom.*

Translated into a technique for helping you create ads and write copy, this means:

a) that you should look at your list of products or services—the things you want to sell and then:

b) decide how these products or services will be of benefit to your target audience, and:

c) write a headline which incorporates these two things.

For instance, suppose you wish to sell a new type of easy-care flooring to young couples with families. Your headline might read:

"Spilled Milk Is Nothing To Cry Over!"

your sub-head or lead-in to the body copy might be:

"Clean-up is easy with XYZ Floors"

and the illustration would be a smiling young mother wiping up the milk while reassuring her young child. Once you are very familiar with what you are selling, and to whom you are selling it, you may find that writing the headlines for your ads is not really so difficult. Remember to always be perfectly honest, and avoid being "cute."

Next you must write the middle of the ad, or "body copy." The object here is to sell. You have stopped the reader with your headline, so now you must tell him/her why those floors are so great, and what they will do to make life easier, better, or more beautiful. Be careful here. Don't get carried away by your own beautiful prose. Keep your copy short, direct, and simple. You may use phrases, or even single words. For instance, "XYZ Floors are made of vinyl. That's right. Plastic." But do be sure the copy flows from one point to the next, and that it makes sense.

Once you have convinced your audience that they must have whatever it is, ask for the business, and tell them specifically where and how to get the product. If it is on sale, say so, and indicate savings. Give time limits, if there are any. If they get a free gift with a purchase, say so. Any pertinent information should be included, but keep it simple and direct. And be very sure that your name and location and phone number are included.

After you think the ad is complete, go over it again. Read it carefully to be sure you've used the right words to convey your exact meaning. Eliminate any unnecessary wordage. If you've used two adjectives to describe the appearance of the floor, see if you can find one word that does a better job. (If you are not familiar with a good thesaurus, buy one!)

Now, call in your artist, and discuss layout and type styles and pictures, and let him/her do the mechanicals.

Magazine advertising can be an excellent addition to your schedule. You may use magazine ads to supplement a campaign using other media, or alone as a reminder between campaigns. Magazines can also be used for a special purpose, such as establishing your image with a particular target audience. As always, be sure to do your homework, whether you're using a local magazine and paying a minimal price per ad, or a regional edition of a national magazine and paying considerably more.

The purpose of your advertising must be clear in your own mind, and your use of magazine ads should be a firm step in accomplishing your goals. Check the efficiency of the money you spend by checking subscriptions and other factors to be sure you are directing your ads at the proper people. Plan ahead. Try to make each ad you insert better than the last. "Better" means "more results," not "prettier." Any ad that fails to get results is a waste of your money, no matter how lovely everyone thinks it is. Keep in mind that frequency can have an effect with magazine ads just as it does with other forms of advertising. Don't forget that one magazine ad in conjunction with newspaper and radio schedules can make it appear that you are using every medium in town.

Direct Mail Advertising

Direct mail can be a very effective advertising medium for the small budget advertiser. To be really effective, it must be planned as carefully as the biggest newspaper ad or the most complex television spot.

Before you start planning a four-color eight-page brochure to be mailed to everyone in the entire city, stop and think a bit. There are some questions you need to answer before you start designing your direct mail piece. First, what do you expect this mailing to accomplish? In what way will it help you achieve your advertising goals? To whom do you plan to send it? How many do you plan to mail?

All of these are valid questions which must be answered if direct mail is to be part of your advertising campaign.

Perhaps the most important question is: "To whom do you plan to mail it?" All of the other questions are related to this one. Assuming you know who your target audience is, how do you go about finding them? There is one list which should be readily available to you. Your own.

Your Mailing List

It is an invaluable practice to be keeping a list of your customers since the day you opened the doors. Have you? Most businesses overlook this important source of repeat business. Unless you have a store which offers store charge accounts, you may very well have no list at all of your customers. Even a list of those with such accounts is not complete. What about all those people who have come in, bought something, and have written checks, or paid cash, or even used other charge cards?

If you are just going into business (or even if you have been open for a while) start right now to compile your own list of customers. It may take a few minutes of a salesperson's time to write out a receipt bearing a name, address, and perhaps a telephone number. It will take a few more minutes for a secretary to file these names on a daily basis. But that list can be an invaluable tool for gaining repeat business.

Another thing it can do is give you some idea of your actual customer profile. Who are they and where do they live? For instance, if you operate a retail store in the west end of town, your customers may all come from an area very close to your location. Or they may be traveling several miles from another part of town simply because your products or services are superior. Do you know, one way or the other? You ought to know.

If you have already acquired all the business in your immediate area, you may want to concentrate your mailing (or even some of your radio, TV, and newspaper ads) on bringing people from other parts of town to your place of business. You may wish to offer a special incentive to do this, or you may wish to reward regular customers by allowing a discount on a popular item. Whatever your goal, if you are planning on using direct mail, the mailing list is highly important.

Building A Mailing List

If you have no list, there are a number of ways to obtain one. First, there are services which provide such lists. Check the yellow pages for such a firm in your city. Local mailing lists can be composed of specific zip codes, or a list of the home addresses of every doctor/lawyer/nurse in your city. These firms will usually sell you the list, or rent you the use of a specific list for a specific mailing. Many of them will address and mail your piece for you, and some will even do the printing. If you decide to use one of these list houses, be sure to check their quality, just as you would any printer. Don't let your direct mail come out looking like "junk mail"to be deposited in the nearest waste receptacle.

Incidentally, you may hear from everyone you know that they never, but *never*, read junk mail. They hate it, and they wish the post office wouldn't deliver it, since it just goes straight into the garbage. Of course, those same people read record and book club mail from cover to cover. They absorb every word of a mailer containing information about a new specialty item related to their hobbies. They read and buy from seed catalogues, and gift catalogues, and Christmas card catalogues, and "white sale" catalogues from the local department store. That same "junk" mail is an enormously successful advertising medium for many national firms as well as for local ones. Businesses, charities and political campaigners all use direct mail. It can be used by you, as a small business, equally successfully.

For your mailing to work for you and bring results, your list must be composed of those people who make up your prime target audience. The piece must be of good quality, the message must be well-done. There should be some incentive to make people wish to act NOW—to buy the product. Your company or business should be presented at its best.

The First Step

As in other forms of advertising, this may sound very complex at first. It isn't. Start with "first things first," and progress step by careful step. If you have decided you want to do a mailing, write down all the facts you can about the product(s) or service(s) you want to sell. Then decide who needs to know about them. They will probably be much the same people you are trying to reach with your radio commercials. Check on the availability of a mailing house in your city, then talk with them about the kinds of lists available and the costs. If there is no such service in your city, and none of your reps can help with finding a national service with lists for your area, you may need to do your own list.

The best place to start is your own list of past customers. With that in hand, try to decide who else you wish to reach. Check the library for a city directory, which should contain most of the information you will need to complete your list. If you can't use a city directory, you can go to the phone book. Using a map which shows all the streets, you can use the phone book to do one section of your city at a time. If there are local magazines in your area, you may be able to rent or buy a list of subscribers. Or, if worst comes to worst, you can check streets and numbers in a single neighborhood, and send your direct mail piece to every house within that area.

The Headline

Once you have your lists, it is time to consider the piece you will be mailing. Here again, you need to decide on specific goals. Know what you are selling, and have a good idea of how it can benefit the person to whom you are selling it. As you have done in other advertising, you must write a headline that grabs the attention of the reader. It should in some way involve his self-interest. "THE ABC SMOKE ALARM CAN SAVE YOUR CHILDREN'S LIVES" is an example of a headline that tells the reader what is being sold at the same time it shows a benefit. Once you have his attention, you must keep it by being as direct and honest as you can be. Your body copy should be to-the-point, giving more features of the product or advantages of your service. The illustrations you use should always be very closely related to the headline and copy. If you are offering a premium, or a gift, or a discount which is good for a limited time, be sure to be very clear on this. Once you have presented all your facts, in such a way that you have convinced the reader to buy, tell him what he must do to obtain the product.

Getting the Order

Ask for the order. "Mail this coupon today for your free ant farm." (Incidentally, if you are offering a free gift, try to make it something connected with the product or service you're selling. For instance, book ends for a series of books; a pen to go with new stationery, etc.) "Call now for your free consultation appointment." "Send in the postage-paid card now for your free brochures." Whatever the action you wish your audience to take, ask them to do it, and tell them how to do it. Make it easy to do it.

Determining Size and Format

Once you have your copy written, consult with your artist and printer on the design of the mailing piece. For almost any small business, a sheet of 8½′ × 11″ typing paper can offer an almost infinite number of possibilities. You can use one side of it and type out a letter. You can use two sides and sell two or three products. You can fold it in half and make a four-page brochure. You can fold it in thirds, and have six pages to work with. You can fold it in half and then fold up the inside bottom yielding a folder with a pocket into which you can insert smaller sheets. Toss ideas around with your artist until you come up with a size and format which lends itself to your plans.

Consider paper stocks and ink colors. Black on white is probably the least expensive. But color adds excitement and prestige. Perhaps you can use a good quality colored paper stock with black ink plus one color ink on one side, and black plus another color on the other side.

Use of Color

While we're discussing color in direct mail, it may be an excellent time to talk a little further about the use of color in your entire scope of advertising. First, billboards, bus and taxi cards are nearly always in two or more colors. They attract more attention that way. But how about your magazine and newspaper ads, and your direct mail peices? Do they need to be four-color to be effective? Not always.

Generally speaking, it depends on what you are selling, as well as the goals you are trying to reach. To look at magazines first; there are some products or ideas that can only be sold effectively through the use of four-color ads. Pick up almost any national magazine and you'll see what I mean. An ad selling a new color of lipstick or nail polish would be useless in black and white; so would an ad selling a new kind of carpet that comes in many shades; so would most fashion ads. If the product you are selling can only be sold through the use of color, you will need to use it.

In a newspaper ad, the same thing does not necessarily hold true. For one thing, since newspsper is printed on a very poor quality stock, a four-color ad does not convey the same feeling the ad might produce if printed on heavy, glossy magazine stock. However, if you need to add some excitement to a newspsper ad, you can usually add one or two colors of ink, besides black, to the ad, to generate more readership.

Check with your paper, or the local magazine you plan to use, for the costs of adding one or more colors of ink to the normal black.

You may find that the addition of one or two colors is not beyond your budget for the ads, allowing you to give a little extra emphasis where it's needed. An expensive four-color ad is justified only if both your budget and goals will make it the most effective way to go.

Color Alternatives

Your direct mail piece can also be made to look more colorful if you will consider these alternatives to four colors. First, the alternatives of colored stock and inks, mentioned above. Next, if your purpose justifies the expense, you may want to create a piece with one or more "inserts." The main piece, a folder of the necessary size, can be in one color stock, with two or more colors of ink. The inserts could be each a different color, either related to or contrasting with the folder. The inks could be the one or two colors plus black that you are already using. Keep in mind that photographs, known as "half-tones," reproduce better if the ink is either black or a color dark enough and strong enough to bring out the necessary details. A chat with your artist, or with the printer, can open up a world of possibilities for use of color in your direct mail pieces without necessarily costing you as much as a four-color ad might cost.

Your direct mail piece may be anything from a business letter on your letterhead, to a four-color brochure with inserts and return envelope, to an invitation on formal notepaper. Whatever form it finally takes should be consistent with your original objective, and with the impression you wish to create. If you are opening a branch bank in a new neighborhood, the formal invitation may be just what you need. If you are selling a special line of women's shoes, you may choose to use illustrations (either art or photos) of the different style, price, and size information. You would aim your copy toward the fashion-conscious woman. If you are selling carpet, you may want to include a sample or an offer of free decorating service. Whatever you are selling, your direct mail advertising should be designed to get results.

This doesn't mean the idea or format has to be dull. There can be great value in surprise, or in unusual uses of everyday objects to attract attention or to make a special point. Consider the single penny: "a penny for your thoughts," "a penny saved is a penny earned," "save the pennies and the dollars will take care of themselves," "penny candy is rare today, but the service your parents got in the country store can be yours at...." "pennies from the piggy bank can buy...."

If you are a bank, you might devise a mailer inviting people to save with you—a mailer made of stiff cardboard, tabbed and slotted, or cut to be folded and glued by the recipient into a piggy bank for a small child.

A photography studio might design an envelope resembling a passport folder, with the copy message: "your passport to perfect portraits" on a slip of paper inside.

Watch your own mail for a few weeks for other ideas. Keep your mailing piece in good taste, and keep the quality as high as possible (or as high as is necessary to convey the appropriate feeling for the particular product). The following are two examples of direct mail packages. One is quite elaborate, while the other should be within the means of most small businesses.

Figure 35. Elaborate direct mail campaign.

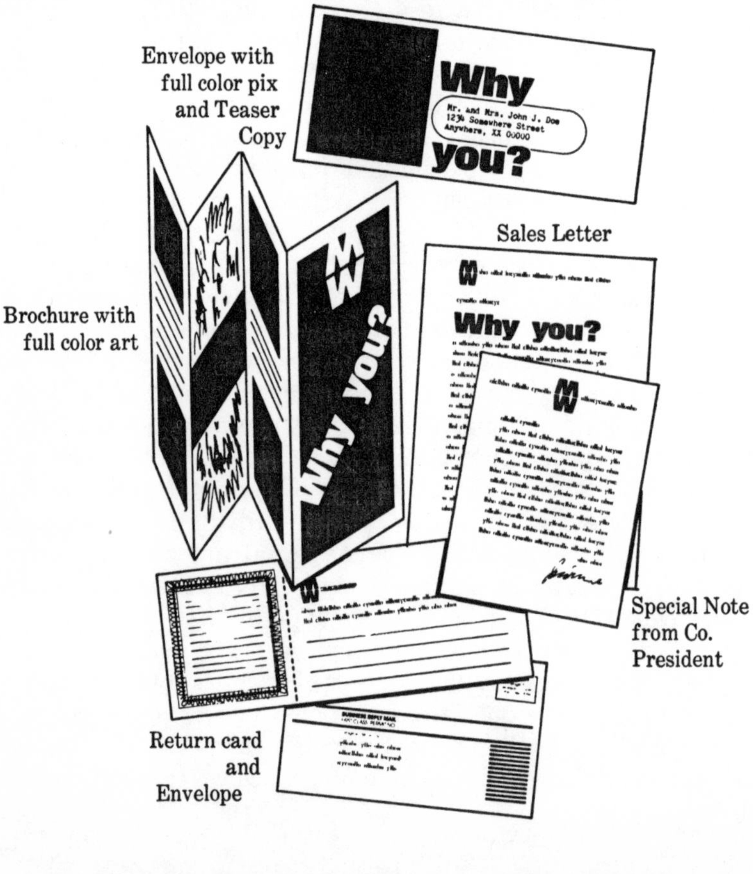

Envelope with full color pix and Teaser Copy
Why
Mr. and Mrs. John J. Doe
1234 Somewhere Street
Anywhere, XX 00000
you?
Sales Letter
Why you?
Brochure with full color art
Why you?
Special Note from Co. President
Return card and Envelope

Figure 36. Simple direct mail campaign.

Envelope with
Teaser Copy

Sales Letter

Reply Card
and
Return
Envelope

When you are planning a direct mail campaign and you have your list, you ought to think a bit about how best to use it. Direct mail has one advantage over some other forms of advertising. If you can get the recipient to open your envelope, you will have his undivided attention for as long as you can hold his interest. This is one of the reasons why direct mail is so effective. Another reason is the fact that he can, if he wishes, lay it aside until he has time to read and absorb it. Still another is the ability to say everything and anything you feel is important, using as many words or pictures as necessary. There are several ways you can use these positive factors.

1. You can mail a single piece a single time to everyone on your list, after a week of broadcast ads telling them it's coming.

2. You can mail the same piece to the same people at a later time,

perhaps with just a change in the envelope. This allows you to save art and printing charges.

3. You can send a series of mailings, on one topic or several, within a short period of time, thus getting your name, logo, address, phone number, and product line in the hands of those to whom it can be of benefit. You also establish enough frequency to increase your recognition among your target audience.

The possibilities for use of direct mail techniques by you as a small advertiser are virtually endless, bounded only by your imagination and the rules of the Postal Service. A simple idea can add greatly to the results you obtain from spending your advertising dollars. Some examples of ideas:

- *a copy of your billhead with the words "PAID IN FULL" beside a free gift item*

- *a four-color eight-page brochure*

- *an (apparently) hand-written note*

When using direct mail, do be cautious. Don't spend all your money in this medium, unless that is the only way you can advertise effectively. Use direct mail as a supplement to your other advertising, a means of communicating directly with your prime target audience in the comfort of their homes, in a highly personalized manner. Make your design the best you can come up with, keep your ad copy clean and always honest, live up to any promises you make. Tabulate your results for each direct mail campaign. You may find that judicious use of direct mail can boost your sales and your recognition. Consult with your post office for ways of making the actual mailing cost as low as possible, and be sure to include costs in your budgets, rather than taking money from another medium.

Billboards And Bus Cards

Two other forms of advertising are "outdoor advertising" and "transit advertising." Outdoor can be billboards, or displays of moving lights which convey messages. Billboards are by far the most common form of outdoor advertising. They can be an effective addition to your planning.

There are good ways to use billboards, and bad ways. Many people look at the enormous size of a billboard, compared with a newspaper ad, and decide they can certainly put all the copy they want in such a tremendous space. Not so. For all its size, a billboard must be read and absorbed in very few seconds. This is someone who is also watching traffic, perhaps talking with another person, and may even be listening to the radio. For the most part, billboards are rather garish-looking—at least the effective ones are garish-looking.

Success With Billboards

To be successful, a billboard can seldom contain more than one product identification, one reason for the reader to purchase, and maybe a location where it may be purchased. Five to a maximum of ten words is a good guideline when you design a billboard. A very simple illustration, in very bright, clear colors may be added, but that should be all. Subtleties are for your four-color magazine and direct mail ads. Billboards should usually have one to three colors, and they should be very bright.

National companies and large chain stores, for instance, have found that using a billboard showing in conjunction with other media can greatly increase product awareness and demand. Normally, billboards are sold in a number of ways. The most frequent uses are in showings of one to twelve months. This means that a certain number of boards in various locations around the city are devoted to one client for the contracted period of time. Some boards are illuminated for night reading, some are not. Some types of contracts allow the client's boards to be moved from spot to spot within the city during a six- or twelve-month showing. Sometimes, you may buy one or two boards in special areas, such as on a street approaching your place of business.

Be sure you understand what is available in your city, and what the costs will be. Some boards are painted, some are posters, and the costs are different for each. Some annual contracts allow you to change copy on your boards one time after the original copy goes up, at no additional charge. You should discover, too, whether the company will repair boards damaged by weather.

A billboard campaign can be a very great help if you are trying to introduce a new product or establish a logo, or supplement your other advertising. Most billboard companies try to locate boards in heavy traffic areas, preferably near stoplights or in other areas where people driving cars will have a chance to read and absorb the messages. This cannot always be done. You may have no choice at all in locations for your particular boards. If you are going to use them, keep your message very simple.

Let's assume you have a new type of carpet available that not only wears forever, it also kills fleas and ticks. This makes the carpet a great bargain for pet owners. You need to do two things with your advertising. First, establish the name of this remarkable carpet. Then tell people where they can buy it.

Your print ads can be quite specific in showing the beauty of the carpet, as well as fairly detailed with description explaining what it does. Your billboards, on the other hand, should be very simple. But keep enough of the style of the other ads to help remind people that this is the product they read about just last week. (Incidentally, if you use television, any of the elements from print should also be used in your TV ads, just as you will use them on your billboards.) A billboard for the fantastic carpet that kills fleas might read:

Figure 37. Sample of billboard copy.

If the logo the manufacturer has devised for use with this carpet is a picture of the carpet, showing several of the colors, and a dog scratching, or a dead flea, you might use that logo as your illustration for the board, placed between the lines of type shown above. This kind of simplicity assures you that your message will be read. If you have the same message on a number of billboards around town as well as other advertising pushing the same logo, location, and message, you should begin to see some results. You may not get people coming in and asking for the carpet by name, but you should get a lot of inquiries about "that carpet that kills bugs." Eventually, if you do enough advertising over a long enough period of time, people will begin to remember the brand name as well as what the carpet does.

Billboards can be an excellent medium for the small advertiser, but they do have some limitations. Their use should be weighed against their cost, what the object is in using them, and how they can add to the efficiency of your advertising.

Bus Cards

Bus cards are a form of "transit" advertising, as are subway cards and taxi cards. These are the billboard-like cards you see on the sides and rear of buses, on the rear of taxis, and inside buses and subways. They are a fairly useful form of advertising, if their limitations are kept in mind.

First, remember that any message on the outside of a moving vehicle is likely to blur after a second or two. Therefore, these messages should be kept very short and simple. Illustrations should be kept to a minimum. The cards inside the bus or subway, on the other hand, may be visible to a passenger for ten or twenty minutes or so. Therefore, you can put more information on these cards. Remember to use type large enough to be read at a distance of several feet.

Your transit advertising should be kept in tune with the advertising in the other media you are using. The frequency with which your target audience hears or sees your message will affect the results you get from your advertising. In any case, whatever the medium you use, repetition is very important. Except for direct mail, which may absorb all of the recipient's attention for a moment or two, advertising is always in the position of competing for the attention of the person you are attempting to reach. Therefore, if some elements of your newspaper ad are included in your magazine ads, billboards, or on your bus cards, you will probably find your message sinks in a little faster, and perhaps sticks a little longer.

There have been cases where an advertiser ran a television campaign for three months, switched to radio for three months, and then started a newspaper campaign, using some of the same art or type from the TV spots. When asked what ad made them come in, customers would frequently say "TV" when there hadn't been a spot on television for six full months. The newspaper ad recalled the television spot to mind. But the TV ad was remembered, not the newspaper ad.

Help in Designing Your Outdoor Advertising

Advertising on billboards or transit advertising can be useful, but it is not normally something you can design on your own. It is a good idea, if you are going to use it, to consult with a rep from the company with which you are dealing, your artist and/or the resident artist with the billboard company.

Your boards need to be designed and laid out to scale, to insure that everything will be in proper proportion for the size of the board. Colors must be chosen for the background, for the type, and for any illustrations you plan to use.

Here are a few ground rules that may help you, but keep in mind that you will probably have to rely very heavily on the expertise of the company with which you are dealing, until you have more experience in this type of design.

1. Words on the board should be at least twelve inches high. If you have secondary words, make your major words even larger than twelve inches.

2. Keep your illustrations very simple. They will appear almost crude when compared with the art for print ads, but this is necessary.

3. Choose your colors very carefully. Be sure they are quite pure and very bright. This is no place to be subtle. Red on white, white on red, black on yellow, yellow on black, are all good at stopping the eye. However, red on black may not be good, since the black may

dull the red somewhat. Ask to see samples of some boards the company thinks are good, and note the color combinations.

4. Try to use some elements you are currently using in other advertising, whether they are logos, type styles, or slogan lines.

5. KEEP THE COPY TO A MINIMUM.

If you are having trouble deciding whether or not outdoor or transit advertising could be of assistance in accomplishing your goals, take a ride around your city. Look at the billboards. Notice designs, colors, and copy. Think about how much of your own personal recall and opinion of products or companies is currently (or has been in the past) influenced by the billboards or bus cards you see every day. Note the frequency with which national brands are advertised on billboards. Then spend a little time thinking about the product or image you are trying to sell.

Can you come up with five words and a design which is striking enough to increase recall? Can outdoor or transit advertising complement the advertising media you are already using? Does your budget permit the scheduling of enough boards or cards over a sufficient period of time to be effective?

Use of outdoor or transit advertising can help you, certainly. But be very sure that your budget permits it, and that you use the space wisely in order for it to be an efficient method of advertising.

Recap

Since we've discussed so many different media in one place, perhaps we should re-think them a bit. First, magazine ads can be a good place to spend some portion of your money, but they should be very carefully tied in with your other advertising in order to obtain the best possible results. For the most part, you should restrain your use of magazines to local or regional publications if you are a local business. This is so that your ads will reach your specific target audience. Be very careful to research the circulation and make-up of the readers of any magazine you consider. If you have a special product which can be sold to people not in your local area, you might consider the regional editions of the national magazines. Write to the advertising department of the magazine in question. They will be more than happy to put you in touch with the proper rep in your region.

There are also the special interest magazines. Remember that carpet that killed fleas? There are an enormous number of pet owners and kennels who subscribe to the various "doggy" magazines. Check with a local kennel club for names and addresses. This technique for reaching a very specific audience outside your immediate geographical location is limited only by whatever product you sell, and by your ability to dig out the information you need. Since we have assumed that you are a small business operating within one city, for the most part you will not need this information. If you do, check with your library. Normally, they will be able to discover all sorts of information on magazines being published for special interest groups.

Keep in mind that direct mail can be useful, but be sure you know to whom you are sending it. Also be sure you know what you are trying to sell them. Make carefully-considered decisions on the design and final appearance of your direct mail ads. Remember that your major objective should be to get the recipient to *ACT NOW*.

Outdoor and transit advertising should be related to your other advertising and used as an additional means of identifying specific products or services. These ads are very simple. They are colorful. And they should fit within your budget.

For the most part, all four of these forms of advertising can be considered additions to the budget of the small advertiser. They can help, certainly. If they are properly planned and designed and executed, they can add dimension and effectiveness to your ad campaign. If your budget is limited, however, try to be sure that your major objectives are met before you use these media.

The direct mail techniques we have been discussing here are aimed primarily at a local geographical area—your city or surrounding counties—but many of the skills needed to produce mailings of this type are used in national mailings.

If, for instance, you are a small manufacturer, rather than a retailer, and you would like to send a mailing to dealers in other states, you may rent or buy lists of such dealers, just as you can local lists, from direct mail houses. There are several companies across the country who supply such lists.

After you have your list, the design and printing and mailing techniques are similar. You will probably wish to be very careful to see that your letter or brochure and order blanks are the best quality you can possibly afford. It doesn't make any sense to spend the cost of postage, art, and production if the piece you mail is too poor in quality to bring results.

Remember, in a national mailing, you will be competing with the big guys—the people who sell by direct mail exclusively—on an equal basis. A local mailing, while it should be the best you can afford, and at least of sufficiently good quality to make the proper impression, has one thing going for it. It comes from a neighbor. Someone whose reputation the consumer can check, or already knows about, sent the letter. A national mailing is going to complete strangers, and the first impression may be the only one you get. Make it the best impression you can.

Chapter 11
Co-op,
Trade-out, And
Miscellaneous

Cooperative Advertising

If you are a retail business selling a product or several products manufactured by a larger company, you may be able to take advantage of co-op advertising. Co-op is "cooperative," and means just what it sounds like. In many cases, manufacturers will assist you with your local advertising costs, if your ads adhere to their rules. This means you can do more advertising, frequently at less cost to you.

The only problem with using co-op money is the fact that you must document the ads. For some reason, many retailers consider this an enormous bother and won't use the co-op money available to them. It's hard to figure out why. All they have to do, in most instances, is request certain documents from the newspaper or radio or television stations, and send them along to the manufacturer. It normally takes about ten minutes and the price of a postage stamp. This is a small price to pay for the invaluable assistance.

For instance, if you are just starting out and have earned some co-op money, you can put it back into your advertising budget. Use the money to increase your business, at which point you may earn more co-op money. This goes back into the budget, and so on. This allows you to grow faster than you might be able to on your own.

How A Co-op Arrangement Works

Normally, co-op works in one of two ways. Some manufacturers will allow you so much money off on your next purchase of their products, after your purchases have reached a certain level. The second method is also based on your purchases, but works differently. The manufacturer wants you to advertise. He offers to pay 25% to 100% of your advertising space or time costs in approved media. That is, if you plan to advertise a specific brand name object of some sort in the newspaper, the manufacturer may well repay you half the cost of the ad. As you can see, if you were planning on a $500 newspaper ad, co-op use could allow you to run two ads of that size at no more expense to you. This should increase your traffic and sales. Let's look at some of the rules that are common among companies who offer co-op advertising.

Newspaper/Magazine (Print) A company offering to repay part of your newspaper costs usually insists that you divide the space into certain percentages. That is, if you are running an ad, from 25% to 50% of the ad will have to be devoted exclusively to their product and names, logos, descriptions, and so forth. The remaining portion of the ad can then be used for your purposes, whether for describing your store or location, or establishing your logo. What you will not be able to do, in most cases, is advertise a competing product in the other part of the ad.

Remember the Crazy Carpet that killed fleas? You might very well do a newspaper ad which describes that carpet fully, and in the other space describe how your company would take great care in installation, give directions to the store, and directions on how to order the carpet. You probably could not advertise another brand name of carpet in the same ad. Aha, you think, all I have to do is send them a proof of the ad, using their copy as directed, and then change it before it runs, adding XYZ carpet.

Nope. For the most part, in order to receive your money, you will have to send Crazy Carpet the following:

1. Two tear sheets of the ad(s)—These are two full pages from each paper that ran the ad, showing the name and dateline of the paper, and the full ad *as it ran.*

2. A copy (sometimes two copies) of the actual bill for space costs. Sometimes the bill must be notarized, sometimes it must be marked "Paid," and sometimes the brand name of the product must be shown on the bill. That is, if your newspaper bill looks like this one, note where the product I.D. (identification) will be:

Date	Paper	Description	Lines	Cost	Totals
9/17	Morn.	Sale;CrazyC.	500	.36	——

Somewhere on the bill will be identification of the ad.

Furthermore, there is normally a time limit. Most companies that pay co-op have cut-off dates. If you have earned co-op dollars in the amount of $500 from January to June of one year, you will usually have to spend and verify the expenditure within the following six-month period of July through December. If you do not use it within the specified time, you will probably lose it. Also, if you run an ad, you have to send in your tear sheets and copies of the billing within thirty days of the date the ad ran.

Special Requirements in Co-op Deals

Most companies who pay co-op at all will pay for ads in your city newspaper. However, magazines may be a little different. Some companies will pay for any magazine ad, just as they do for newspaper ads. Others will require a copy of the magazine, a rate card, and perhaps some information about who is subscribing and how many are subscribing. They want this information *before* you run an ad for which you want to receive co-op monies. If the magazine is really one that reaches your target audience and is reputable, you should have no trouble getting the approval you need. Take the time to do it, since you never know when you may wish to use that approval.

Another thing you should be aware of is copy requirements. If a company is allowing you money for co-op print ads, they may very well send you a packet of ads which you may use for this purpose. These ads are usually ready for reproduction by the newspaper and come in various sizes. They will have product identification, descriptive copy, a place for a price, and a space for you to insert your company name and address. If you use these ads, you will find that the manufacturer is getting the major part of the space (perhaps as much as 75% to 80% of the space of the actual ad) for which he is paying you 50% of the price of the space, or less. You may certainly use these ads as they arrive if you wish. They are normally quite good, and may be tied very closely to whatever national advertising the manufacturer is running.

Making the Most of Co-op Money

To get more mileage out of your ad dollars, however, check the fine print in the co-op agreement. If it says that the company will pay you 50% of the space cost as long as the company product has at least one-half of the space used, then give the company exactly one-half of the space in your ad and *use the rest for yourself.* This is an excellent way to get mileage out of your ad dollars. Use of co-op will allow you to run larger ads, which may get you more attention. You can push your company image and logo at the same time you are selling a particular product.

To avoid problems, try to keep the ads fairly divided into their half and your half, so that when you send in your tear sheets, the person checking them will have as little trouble as possible.

Co-op in Broadcast Advertising

Besides newspaper and magazine co-op, some companies will pay for all or part of your broadcast time costs. Again, you will have to check the fine print for rules, but most companies who pay co-op will require the following:

1. An affidavit or notarized statement from the station showing the date and exact time the spots ran, the title of the sponsor, the cost per spot, and the total cost. The sponsor I.D. may include your name, but should definitely have their name. That is, if you are "The Store" selling XYZ Carpet, the affidavit would show "Store/XYZ Carp." or some other variation which clearly indicates what ran.

2. A copy of the script which ran, also notarized by the station. At times, you will have to have a tape number, if the spot was recorded instead of live. But you will need to be able to say exactly what spot ran and when. Fortunately, the stations must keep a log of what runs when, and they will send you a notarized statement about your spots if you need it.

Sometimes a company will request that you send scripts or storyboards to them for approval prior to actual airing of the commercials. If the script or storyboard is approved, they will assign it a number, and that number will then need to appear on the copies of the affidavits or notarized bills from the station. None of this is really difficult for you to provide, and it may mean a considerable addition to your advertising budget.

Newspapers, magazines, television and radio stations will be glad to provide the correct information and documentation for you to send in to collect your co-op. The information is already on their records. However, be sure to tell them *ahead of time* that this ad or spot schedule is co-op. The broadcast media will need to write your contract in such a way that the name of the co-op advertiser will appear on the daily logs.

Also, if the people in charge of continuity at the stations know that they will be required to supply copy or tape numbers for co-op purposes, they are usually slightly more careful in keeping track of it. This is more difficult than it may sound. For instance, a radio station may well carry eighteen minutes of commercial time every hour for twenty-four hours, seven days a week. The stations normally send out bills once a month. Sure, the log must say what ran when, and certainly your copy must have been there at that time, and supposedly the station will keep a copy of all scripts for a length of time. However, one person is handling perhaps 400 different spots (that's the minimum for the above example of eighteen commercial minutes in each hour of twenty-four, considering those eighteen minutes were actually divided into thirty- or ten-second spots) in one day. With that many different commercials, the person may not have a clear memory of the spot you ran on September 5th and 6th.

Your rep will handle all of this for you, if you remember to tell him/her that a particular schedule is a co-op. The contract will be "flagged" or marked in some way, and the appropriate people at the station will know to send the following along with your bill:

A. at least two copies of the bill itself; one for you and one for the co-op company. They will show number of spots, cost, and sponsor I.D. The bills will be appropriately notarized.

B. two copies of each "live" script that ran in the above time periods, also notarized.

C. if the spots were taped, the tape number and identification should appear on the notarized bill.

If you don't tell your rep ahead of time that you will be needing this information, you are likely to have to wait a bit for it. This delay may mean you lose your co-op money if you can't meet the deadlines for submission. Save yourself some time and money, and make sure to tell ahead of time.

Co-op is a great way to add from 25% to 50% to your annual ad budget. This is if you are fortunate enough to deal in a product or products upon which the manufacturer is willing to spend some money. However, you must run the ads as stated, and the billing and the scripts must be truthful. The station can lose its license to broadcast if they falsify information of this type, so don't ask them to do it. You may also get in trouble, and the hassle isn't worth it. Occasionally, an advertiser will run an extensive schedule, and then ask his ad person or station rep to give some verification for co-op, stating that certain spots were run at certain times. There might not be a record of the spots having run as stated. Most stations will be happy to provide a copy of an old bill, if that will help. However, they will not change the bill in any way. So be sure to tell your reps when you buy the schedule that you'll need co-op verification.

Newspaper and magazine ads, being tangible, are not quite so much of a problem. It's a good idea to require that the paper send you at least three tear sheets of each and every ad you run, whether the ad is co-op or not. That way, you will always have a record for your own use, and tear sheets for co-op will automatically be available. Also, be sure to request either "checking copies" of a magazine in which you run an ad, or tear sheets. Make quite plain to the rep that you must have tear sheets or checking copies for any of your print ads before you will pay their bills. For the same reason, you should try to get all billing from media in duplicate at least. If you can't, be sure you make a copy of each bill for your files.

If you will be using co-op funds to any great extent, it is a good idea to have one person on your staff in charge of gathering and checking all the materials against the requirements of the various companies who will be paying you. It should probably be the same person who will check the contracts for the media in which you place ads, and then checks the bills and pays them. If this person is to be you, so be it. Take the time to request what you need, and as soon as the bills come in, check to be sure you've received all the verification you requested.

In most cases, the broadcast contract will show the co-op request. If the newspaper or magazine issues its own contracts, these may contain co-op information also. However, some print media will require an "insertion order" from you. Any firm which regularly deals with magazine ads will have an insertion order form. You can make your own, using your letterhead, and typing on it the following information. Then run off a number of copies. Always keep a copy of every insertion order you send, in case questions arise later. Your insertion order should show:

Figure 38. Insertion Order

To the publisher of:_____ Date:_____

Address:_____

Please insert the following advertisements for: *(product)*

Size	# Times	Dates of Insertion	Copy

Position preferred:_____

Rate per ad:_____ Discount%_____

BILLING IN DUPLICATE ____ Tear Sheets or ____ Checking Copies

Signed: _____

You may number your orders if you wish, so that your records are easier to keep straight. Also, once the ad has run, you may find it convenient reference to place one copy of each tear sheet with the insertion order. That way, if you run an Easter ad this year, you can check it when Easter rolls around again, and may discover that you can run virtually the same ad.

If you keep records anyway, you should find co-op advertising easy to use. It is a good way to get more out of your advertising dollars. So by all means use it if your business is one which makes such funds available.

Trade-Outs

Sometimes a business can trade the product or service it sells for radio or television time, or newspaper or magazine space. If you sell Superpens, and you need to advertise them in your city, you may be able to work a deal with that magazine whereby you supply them with pens for their use, and they supply you with space for your ad. It all sounds wonderful in theory.

Caution

In practice, you must be very careful indeed. If you wish to trade-out your products or services with a radio station, for instance, be very sure you have a written agreement or contract stating exactly what you will get for your product or service. Radio stations, TV stations, even magazines, tend to consider a trade-out agreement as one where they are giving you their time or space out of the goodness of their hearts. Therefore, you should be grateful for any spot or placement of your ad which they choose to give you. Think about that for a moment.

Suppose you sell lighting fixtures. The radio station needs thirty of your fixtures, plus the professional installation only your company can provide. The retail value of each fixture is $100, and the installation charge is normally $15 per fixture. Therefore, the total value of the deal (from your end) is $3450. That should buy you a reasonable number of radio spots. You should be able to place those spots in all time periods, wherever they will aid your advertising objectives. Many stations will assume the attitude that you are being given "free" spots and try to insist that your spots run whenever they have some free time.

Don't buy it. If you're going to trade, trade value for value. You didn't place those new fixtures where you thought they ought to go, but where the station thought they would do the most good. By the same token, you should be able to place your spots where you think they will do the most good. If the station attempts to tell you anything else, you would probably be better off to charge them cash for those fixtures, then turn around and spend the cash on the station. This would insure that your spots run where you want them to run.

Getting It in Writing

Trade agreements seem to be declining slightly in popularity, perhaps due in part to misunderstandings. To avoid problems, you ought to get all details of the agreement in writing, signed by someone at the station, and signed by you. Be quite firm in insisting that your spots be scheduled where you want them, or that your magazine ad will not be buried. Also, keep in mind that trade-outs do not normally include art-work or production costs, merely time or space charges. You will have to do the ad or spot yourself.

Trade-outs can be a way of using the major media, even if your cash budget is extremely low. However, do be sure you clearly under-stand exactly what is involved before you jump in. If you can take ad-vantage of trades to build your business, go ahead and do it. But do stay alert to what you are getting in return for what you are giving. Using trade-out, treat the money that is available to you (actually space or time) as though it were coming out of your budget, not as though it's a free schedule.

For a small business, use of co-op money, sometimes combined with trade-outs, can mean a great deal more advertising on a very small budget, which is certainly all to the good. Have one person at your busi-ness be in charge of these things, and use them correctly. Your adver-tising can be spread out over more different media, or for longer schedules, than you might afford on your own.

Miscellaneous

Before we go into the planning of your budget, let's look at some of the ideas and pitfalls, and thinking patterns, that will help you make the most of every dollar you spend on advertising.

For instance, if you have doubts about which of the two ads or com-mercials to use, there is a way to find out which works the best for you. Test them.

Testing Your Ads

If you have two newspaper ads, perhaps both containing a coupon, and the appearances are different, before you place the ad for a long-term schedule, run a very short test schedule.

Suppose you have two papers in your town, a morning and an eve-ning. Run both ads in both papers, and see which attracts the most results. You can "key" the ads if you wish, by placing a tiny letter or number in one corner of the coupon. Then see which coupon came from which ad and which paper. You can re-test by using the winning ad in different papers, on different days. When you find the ad, and the com-bination of paper and day that does the most good, stick with it for a bit. Keep running that ad until you feel you've obtained the results that indicate a move.

At that point, re-test again. If your budget is too small to do this, at least try to take a survey (perhaps at a shopping center) and ask which ad would make the person read and send in the coupon. Anytime you can pre-test an ad's effectiveness before you embark on a long schedule, you will be wise to do so. You are not trying to find out which ad looks the prettiest, remember. Advertising should never call attention to its own appearance, but to the appearance of the product or service you wish to sell.

Another thing you ought to be aware of is readership of ads. Do by all means get a hold of a "Starch" survey if you can, and go over it carefully. It will reveal information which can be very useful when you are designing print ads. However, here are some thoughts for you to consider. If you are using a photograph as part of your ad, be very sure that the photo is directly related to your headline and the first paragraph of your body copy.

Using Captions

If you use a striking photo that attracts attention, but the headline is unrelated, you will confuse your reader. Also, be sure that the caption to the photo contains the essence of the message contained in the entire ad. Lots of people read captions who don't bother to read ads. If your caption is complete with the name of the product, or a description of the service you are trying to sell, as well as your name, and any benefit the reader may expect from his/her purchase of this product or service, your message will reach the reader, even though only the fifty or sixty words under the picture might be read.

Using Subtitles

Also, if you are using a lot of very descriptive copy, it is usually a good idea to break up the appearance of so much type by keeping your paragraphs short, and using subtitles or other means to keep the reader's attention. Be sure to tell the reader, or the audience, (if you're using broadcast), what the benefits will be for buying this product. Before anyone will buy anything, he/she must be made to see why he/she should do so. You won't help make this decision by being general, or by using flowery terms.

If you install wallpaper, for instance, you may wish to sell the fact that you give excellent installation. Don't just say that; say that your expert installers will clean and prime the walls properly, that they will take care to be sure the pattern matches exactly, that they will clean up any mess they make, and that you personally will come by to inspect one week after the job is completed, to make sure there are no problems. "Expert Installation" means nothing; facts do. All your advertising should contain enough facts to tell your target audience why they should buy whatever it is that you're selling; even a 1/12 of a page ad in a magazine should contain a copy line which tells why readers should shop at your store.

No matter what kind of advertising you are doing, there are two questions you should ask yourself. First, "What will it cost me?" and second, "What results can I expect if I spend this money?" The results should outweigh the cost.

Grand Opening Events

Let's look at an example. If you are a small business, and you are just opening your doors, you may be advised to have a "Grand Opening" or, at the very least, a party of some sort to which you will invite all those people you wish to impress with the fact that you are now in business. Think about that for a minute. A grand opening can certainly attract a crowd of people to your place of business. However, you should ask yourself whether your staff can handle, say, 500 customers in one day. If you are planning little gifts, or food, to be given away, how much will it cost you to feed all those people? Will the fact that you are offering all these enticements cause them to buy anything? Of course, you may wish to let your friends and neighbors (who will probably become customers) know that your doors are open. Later you may want to have a tremendous sale, but these things should be very carefully planned. First, be sure that your place of business and your staff are fully prepared for the event. If you have just opened your doors, it is usually a good idea to wait from two to four weeks before you plan an event of any great size. That way, the staff will be very familiar with the business and the products you sell, you will know that the water fountain and the toilets and the front door all work as prescribed, your business cards with the wrong address will have been reprinted correctly (let's hope this never happens!), and your sign will be up.

All of this may sound terribly silly, and of course you wouldn't open the doors until you are ready, but.... I've seen it happen more than once. And it isn't much fun, besides giving all those customers a bad first impression of a vulnerable new business.

So take your time with such events. Be very careful what type event you plan. For instance, if you have a number of investors, close friends, and advisors, you may very well wish to have them in for a little welcoming view of your business. Fine. Have it after hours one evening. Make it a wine and cheese party, invite the staff to be a part of it, and enjoy it. Incidentally, you'll score a lot of points if you avoid making the secretary or sales manager the one in charge of the party. They like to feel like guests, too, and to feel that introductions to the investors won't be made just at the moment they have to serve the cheese. If you can't afford a caterer, ask your spouse or one of your spouse's friends (or perhaps hire someone from a part-time agency). You will need to buy wine and the cheese and crackers, and arrange for glasses and so forth, but the helpers will do the actual set-up and serving. Pay them minimum wage, and be sure they know where everything is before the party starts.* A caterer is better, but if you must watch the pennies, this way will work, as long as you are quite explicit about under-age people being hosts or hostesses, not servers. Have soft drinks available for them, as well as for those guests who may not care for wine. This type of small celebration gives your investors and others concerned the chance to look over your business, without it costing you an arm and a leg.

On the other hand, suppose you are ready for the world to beat a path to your door. Fine. That's the time to have your "Grand Opening" celebration. Advertise as much as your budget permits, in order to attract as many customers as you can. There are all sorts of ways you can do this, but try to be careful to keep in mind the kind of image you are trying to achieve in the minds of your audience. For instance, if you sell terrifically exclusive giftware (the kind where each piece is displayed on its own pedestal with appropriate lighting) you probably don't want to offer hot dogs and balloons for the kids, nor have a radio station playing rock music on the premises. In such a case, you may use radio, television, and newspaper advertising, but you may also use a

*I am not recommending that under-age people serve alcoholic beverages. But they can be sure that the empties are disposed of, clear used glasses away, clean up ashtrays and cracker crumbs, bring out and serve more cheese, fill the cracker trays, and bring new bottles of wine to the table for your attention.

carefully selected direct mail list, inviting a very specific target audience to a "showing" or "grand opening viewing" of your product line. On the other hand, if you are a hardware store, with everything for the home handyman, you may indeed want activities and food for the kids (maybe even a person on hand to supervise them), while mom and dad look over the store and talk with your helpful salespeople (who, incidentally, know all that anyone needs to know about the products and services you offer). If you were opening a record store, and wished to attract the attention of every teenager and young adult in your market area, you might use the rock music stations, with announcers and music in the store. Offer soft drinks and potato chips or French fries free with any purchase.

Be Prepared

Any of these introductions to your store can be very valid ways of getting your name in front of the people whose business you wish to attract. But be sure that your budget and your staff are ready for them. Don't have a grand opening celebration which brings hundreds of people through in one day, unless you are prepared for this. Lack of such preparation can mean that many of the people who come in expecting to buy go away angry, simply because at the time they could come, your staff was too busy to pay them any attention. At the very least, have one or two people who do nothing but greet new arrivals and steer them toward the area of their major interests. Another person can be available to handle problems which may arise. An angry customer spouting off in loud tones about the cause of his/her discontent can ruin the feeling you've worked so hard to create, and cause you to lose business from other people in the store. No one wants to deal with a store or business that can't seem to satisfy its customers.

Be Well-stocked

Another pitfall to avoid is the lack of stock. If you use a full-page newspaper ad in addition to other media to advertise the fact that your grand opening will feature special items at big savings, do be sure you have plenty of the items in the store. It is very disappointing to visit a new business at seven in the evening (that being the only time you have) only to discover the item you coveted has been sold out. It is bad enough when this happens at a regular sale put on by an established business. When it happens during the introduction of a new business, it can quite easily succeed in turning customers off so much that they never come back. If you advertise it, be sure you have it.

There is a reason for all this care you will take. From the moment you open your doors, your business is dependent on the number of people you can attract and hold as customers. Whatever your business or service, you must have people. It is very important, therefore, that you do not turn them off the first time they walk through your doors. National advertising makes people familiar with new products, brand names, quality, packaging, and so forth. If you sell such things, your major thrust in local advertising will probably be based on two things:

a) the services you offer, or the reasons people should shop at your place of business, and

b) any special pricing you can offer as an enticement.

So be very sure that whatever you advertise, you can make good on. This holds true as long as you are in business and (therefore) in competition with other businesses. It is most especially important when you begin the competition by opening the doors. Customers who have been dealing with one store for many years are not likely to be too upset if they have to wait a day or two for something they need. However, if they have come to your new place to buy an item, and you don't have it, they will probably go back to the older store and never darken your step again. Make good on the promises you make.

Incidentally, before you advertise at all, you need to think of reasons why people should buy your products or shop at your store. National advertising has established the names and appearances of many thousands of products firmly in the minds of almost everyone in the country. If you sell them, you probably don't need to add to that kind of advertising. If several other stores in your area sell basically the same product, you may have to offer special incentives to tempt people to buy from you rather than the others. This temptation may range from a discount on the price, to a free gift of some sort, or even to free installation or a six-month inspection. Be sure you have your ideas firmly fixed in your mind before you start planning your advertising, since these reasons are the basis you will use for writing all your ad copy.

Now let's take a brief look at some small businesses, and how they might publicize their goods or services.

Photography   If you are an excellent photographer, and you want to obtain your share of the bridal and family protrait business in your area, your major advertising will probably be newspapers and direct mail. In order to get people to try you for the first time, you may have to offer some sort of special discount, or extra copies of pictures. This offer will naturally be made in your newspaper ads. Also, you may wish to mail a personal letter to the homes of high school students in your area, or to the homes of brides who register with local stores. Such a letter should be on good quality stationery, and personal enough to attract the attention of the bride. You may also wish to volunteer your services to speak to church youth groups, or to high school home economics classes. The initial thrust will be to get your name out in the community, and the main season for your advertising may well be just after Christmas, when the June brides start planning. Radio can be an excellent medium, too, if you make your place sound like the only place where the young women can get the picture they've always dreamed of.

Hardware   There are usually a number of ways such stores can attract attention. Among them are classes for various home repair or building projects, discount certificates mailed to addresses near your place of business, "Helpful Hints for Home Repair" columns included in each radio spot or newspaper ad you run. Hardware stores also usually have a lot of co-op money available, and it is a good idea to use it. However, don't be tempted to use every bit of co-op available, if the expenditure of the money which is not co-op will be more than your budget allows.

Electronics/Home Entertainment   A good way to show people what you have to offer is a direct mail invitation to those people who fit your target audience income designation. The invitation should be mailed in small bunches, with specific dates suggested for an appropriate "personal" showing of the latest equipment. Also, there is the large volume/low price dealer who will from time to time use either full-page ads or magazine inserts in the newspaper, teamed with extensive radio advertising to attract large numbers of buyers. Whichever approach you use, do be sure that your personnel are very knowledgeable about the equipment, so that any question will receive a prompt and accurate answer.

Catalogs   Many retail businesses are finding that a catalog can increase their sales, particularly during special selling seasons such as Christmas, or for the annual "white sale." If you are planning such a catalog, you may wish to consult with an ad agency which handles this type of thing. If you are going to do it yourself, you will need to work very closely with your artist and your printer.

First, you must decide on the objective. Is the catalog to be used solely as a buying guide for your consumers? Or will it also be used by salespeople as a selling tool? In either case, a catalog must be carefully designed in order to be effective.

Let's look at some ideas to keep in mind while you are planning your catalog. The example in this case will be a "white sale" catalog.

1. Group your products logically. That is, sheets all in one section, with accessories such as pillow slips; blankets in another section; towels/washclothes in another. If you have designer items that come in complete sets—sheets, pillow slips, draperies, dust ruffles, rugs—you may wish to devote a page to each separate pattern. You may group them according to rooms, or according to use, but do be careful to see that the grouping makes sense.

2. Design the pages so that the facts about sizes and prices and ordering information are in the same place on each page.

3. Remember that the customer is seeing two pages at once, and design each spread with that in mind.

4. As with the other forms of advertising we have discussed, keep your design clear, simple, and easy to read. Make it easy for your customer to see each product and to find the needed facts.

5. If you cannot afford a four-color catalog, try using a single color to break up the monotony of all black and white. Check with your printer after you know the final number of pages to see if separate groups of pages can be printed with black plus a separate color. If so, you can use this technique to add some excitement. It should not cost you much to change one ink color for each separate group of pages. This way, you can use a color as the heading for each category, or for the information on ordering, or perhaps as background for some of your pictures.

6. Be sure the cover is attractive and "hard-hitting" and that the reader knows immediately that it is a new catalog. People like to read catalogs, and they use them, particularly if the catalog presents new products or offers sale prices on items they may need or use. Even the envelope should indicate the contents, so no one will toss your catalog in the trash without knowing what it is. An interesting thing about catalogs as opposed to direct mail pieces is that people tend to retain catalogs longer. When someone gets a direct mail letter in the mailbox and isn't immediately interested in buying the product advertised, it goes into the trash. When the same person receives a catalog, but cannot attend to it right away, he/she will usually hold on to it to read at a later time.

7. Be sure to include order forms or cards, and even an envelope if you can. Be quite clear in giving the directions about ordering, the time limits (if any), and any pertinent information about payment methods.

8. Make a dummy of your catalog, using the proper paper, envelope, etc. Check with the post office to be sure you have followed all the rules.

9. From the first step to the last, keep in mind that inaccuracies in the catalog can cause hassles you don't need. Proofread everything carefully, at every stage. Have two or three other people proofread at every stage. Double check things such as sizes and model numbers. An "e" instead of an "o" in the word "to" is not a disaster, but an incorrect model number can cause massive problems.

The following is an illustration of the White Sale Catalog mentioned earlier.

Figure 39. Sample catalog.

Group products
according to
use

Design 2 page spread to
go together visually as well
as product relationship

Sizes and prices
grouped for
easy reference

Important information
such as prices should be
emphasized by bold
type of color

Ordering information and
Order Form may be
bound into catalog or
a loose insert

A catalog can be a good tool for the small business. Keep in mind that you must present the information clearly and concisely, that photography can add immeasurably, that all facts must be there where your customers can easily use them to decide on their purchases and to place their orders. If your catalog is more complex than can be covered with this information, you will probably need some professional help in compiling and designing it. You would do well to obtain such help, thus insuring the kind of catalog you want and need, rather than wasting your valuable time and money doing a job that is not going to bring results.

Point-of-Purchase Displays

As a retailer, you may have many of these displays on your floor. They are made of wire, wood, cardboard, or masonite, and they generally hold an attractive display of several products from one manufacturer. They are an important consideration for the small manufacturer, since they may well decide how quickly and easily your salespeople can sell your products to the dealer (retailer) for sale to the consumer. If you fall into this category, and you will be needing either packaging design or point-of-purchase display designs, you will do well to consult with a professional. Design is never an easy task for an untrained eye. In this case, it could mean the life or death of your product line. So it might not be a good idea to try to scrimp and save in this area.

If, on the other hand, you are a retail business of some sort, you may obtain (or be provided with) displays from your various suppliers. They can help your sales if they are well-designed, so don't toss them out without seeing how they could work for you.

Some retailers may wish to create their own displays. For instance, if you are having a sale of some sort, even a sale involving several different products, you may want to create a special display. This could be a table or floor area, which contains the sale items. You may point it up by pasting your newspaper or magazine ad on a piece of board. This prominent display of the ad and the items should be placed where customers can find it quickly, since many of them will be seeking a specific item.

In most cases, if you will need an actual design for a point-of-purchase display, to be coordinated with your products and packaging, my advice would be to engage professional help. You may be able to find books that tell you about it, and that offer techniques, but none of them will be able to turn you into a designer. This is not a good time to try it yourself!

These examples are only a few of the many ways you can advertise or publicize your business or products. You will need to decide on the best strategy to use for your particular business. However, as you should be realizing, there are many things that all small businesses ought to bear in mind. No matter what you are selling, you must know all about it, its good and bad points, and why a customer should buy it, whether it is a product or service. You need to be thoroughly aware of who your customers are, what kind of lives they lead, what their income range is, and what media they watch, listen to, and read. Your advertising can then show a problem this person has, and what your product or service will do to alleviate the problem, or add beauty or convenience to his/her life.

Here are examples of the different types of displays.

Figure 40. Point-of-purchase displays.

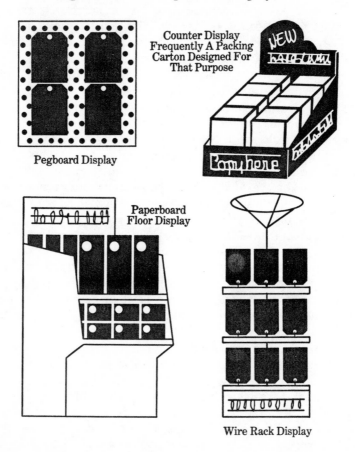

In the next chapter we will discuss how you can work out your own advertising campaign/budget plan. Before we do this, however, you need to be aware of your customers, of your business or service, and of your goals. Now is the time to do any research you have not yet performed. Now is the time to look up and have ready all the information on co-op or trade-out possibilities. Now is the time to gather all the rate cards, rating figures, the mats from your wholesalers. Take the time to gather everything you have available which might contribute to your advertising planning.

Once you start making your plan, you will be using these materials. It is much easier to plan with things if the things are at hand. Get all of your information organized so that retrieval of any specific piece involves only reaching out your hand, not the end of your temper.

Put everything into appropriately-labeled file folders and keep it all together under "Advertising." Then do your planning (with the help of the next chapter), knowing that everything you need will be handy.

Chapter 12
Planning Your Ad Campaign

In this chapter, we will look at the mechanics for planning two types of campaigns. First, a short-term plan for publicizing a sale or special event. The second will be the long-term annual plan for all your advertising. Of necessity, actual budget amounts will be arbitrary selections, since each business or event will use different budgets. However, you ought to be able to apply your own goals and budget to the planning, thus coming up with figures to suit your own needs. In each case, if you have more money available, you will be able to do more advertising. Less money will net less advertising. The basic planning technique remains the same.

Before you actually begin planning any campaign, there are some facts you will have to know. It is a good idea to gather these facts right now, and have them readily available. For the sake of convenience, divide them into two broad categories. First, internal facts, which include:

1. The make-up of your prime target audience.

2. The goal of the sale or special event. Try to confine this to a one- or two-sentence description, including such things as gross sales figures you expect, and the amount of traffic you need to achieve these figures.

3. Your budget for this event. Break it down (if you have co-op dollars available which you plan to use) into figures which show you just how much cash you will be able to spend, how much can be spent on ads for the specific co-op products, and any other pertinent divisions. You will still have a "total" budget of some sort, which is the thing you will be working with.

4. The dates of the event and the products you will be selling, with all applicable information (such as: newspapers mats available, radio or television spots available, prices–both regular and sale). If you don't already have this information, prepare it now. Also, be aware of stock availability, that could pose a problem.

The idea is to get all the information you will need to place, create, and run your advertising together in one place. This includes all the product and store information you have.

The second category is "external" information, and includes:

1. Rate cards for all media you plan to use. Newspaper, radio and television, or any other media which seems or has been proven a good buy.

2. Requirements as to time ahead you will need to place your ads and mechanical requirements for getting the ad in the paper or on the air on time.

3. An easy-to-use calendar. Don't try to use a pocket-size calendar, since it is easy to make mistakes with tiny numbers. Get one of the kind that have one-inch squares for each date, and at least one whole month per page. Two months might be better, but they are hard to find. If you can't locate one, make your own. Draw squares on a piece of paper, and write in the dates. It is a good idea to start six weeks ahead of the event, and go forward through one week after.

4. Call the broadcast media reps you will be using and check on availabilities for the dates you will need spots. In the case of radio, from a week ahead of the date, to the dates themselves. For television, for this type of event, look at perhaps forty-eight hours ahead, through late afternoon of the last day of the sale, if you will be open at night, or late night the day before the sale ends, if you will be open until five p.m.

Once you have all the information at hand, you can begin your planning for this special event. It is usually best to do your work on a schedule so that at any time you will know exactly where you stand, and how much and what is left to do. Below is a list of ideal planning times. This is for convenient reference, and will work in most cases. In retail businesses, however, it is sometimes hard to work this far in advance, since plans can change from week to week. In the beginning, if you can stick to this sort of schedule for your first three or four sales or special events, you will find that when you must later work out such plans in much less time, you have a good basis for gauging how much work is involved.

Six Weeks Ahead: Gather all information. Set dates for sale or event.

Five Weeks Ahead:	Call media reps for availabilities. Set budget. During this week, work out a full plan, how much money is to be spent on which media, and how much per station (if you are using several).
Four Weeks Ahead:	Place all media buys. Begin planning your ads and spots. This means, begin your rough layouts for print ads, and copy themes, and ideas for broadcast.
Three Weeks Ahead:	Check media contracts for accurate placement of your spots. Produce all advertising, setting the mechanicals for any print ads to be done by you or your artist, sending layout to newspapers if they are to produce ads, getting proofs and checking and approving them, finalizing radio and TV scripts, producing and approving final commercials for airing.
Two Weeks Ahead:	Go over all ads and budgets to be sure they are correct. Get ads to media, with special instructions for any particular scheduling which may be necessary.
One Week Ahead:	Double-check products on sale, work with personnel regarding traffic problems which may arise, inform staff of ad schedule so they may be sure to see or hear the ads. If they cannot see the actual ads, show them proofs or copies of scripts so they will know what is being said. Check with your media reps to be sure your schedule will start as planned, and to be sure all media have correct copy.

Unless you are planning to use television, which usually requires this much lead time for production, you may be able to do all of the above in one week, or even less, provided the time you need and the space you need is available. Many retailers work on this week-to-week basis as a matter of habit. However, if you could work this far ahead, and be careful with your space and time buys, and be sure your ads (whether print or broadcast) are the best you can make them, you will probably find that your results will show the benefits of taking this extra care and time.

Next, let's discuss the planning of the budget, or how to spend the money. Get your calendar, and your rate cards, and your total budget figure ready. Be prepared to spend as much as several hours on this, especially the first time or two you do it.

There are a number of things you will already know, before you sit down to plan your media buys. For instance, if there are ten radio stations in your town, and your target audience can primarily be found listening only to three of them, you will know which three stations to look over first. You will know whether the thing you are selling needs the "item and price" kind of ad, or whether it will sell better another way. When planning this kind of event, you will not necessarily look at every station in town, nor at ads every day in the newspaper. You will, instead, look at those stations and papers which are likely to be able to attract the ages and income groups you need as traffic. If you have done your research, you will have this information ready. When you combine it with your budget available for the event, you will know how and where to begin.

The first step in planning the use of the budget is to apportion it correctly within the media you plan to use. If your budget is, say $1500, for a two-day sale, you will need to decide at this point on the following figures.

1. How much will be used for newspaper ad or ads—space costs only?
2. How much will be used for radio time costs?
3. How much will be used for TV, if that is a consideration?
4. How much should be used for production of ads and spots?

These very basic budget divisions should be made at the beginning of your planning. A little later, you will need to plan your specific time and space buys for all media. At this point, you may want to make a plan that looks like the one on the following page. The total budget in this case $2500.

Figure 41. Sample of advance budget plan.

Date	Newspaper Size	Cost	Radio Station	Cost	Total
Wed. 9/10	¼ p. Morn.	$250	QQQQ	$100	
	¼ p. Even.	225	WOOO	200	
			BBBB	150	
					$925
Thur. 9/11	¼ p. Morn.	250	OQQQ	100	
			WOOO	200	
			BBBB	150	
					700
Fri. 9/12	¼ p. Morn.	250	OQQQ	100	
			WOOO	200	
			BBBB	150	
					700
					$2325.00

Production Charges:	Newspaper ad	100
	Radio spots.....................................	75
		175.00
		$2500.00

This type of advance planning with your budget will do two things. First, it will tell you when your ads have to be ready to run and secondly, it will give you an overall view of where your money will be placed, and whether or not you have allocated enough money to do the job properly. Keep in mind that the ads are not going to sell the products. All the ads can do is bring the customers to your door, from which point your sales staff will take over. Therefore, you must design your advertising to bring in as many people as possible, since not everyone will buy. In the example, we have scheduled ads the day before the sale, as well as on the two sale days. However, if money is tight, you may wish to schedule ads the afternoon before the sale, and the first day of the sale only. This will insure enough frequency to gain the attention you need. In general, it is a good idea to talk with the media reps for all the stations you plan to use, and discover how many spots are needed to reach each member of the audience an average of two to three times.

The first time they hear a spot, most of it will not register. The second time they hear it, they may realize they've heard it before. They may realize that there is a sale of wurtzel birds somewhere in town. If they are at all interested, by the time they hear the third spot, they are waiting to hear prices and location and name of the store.

Your newspaper ads should be sure to include this same type of very pertinent information. For a short-term schedule, use the same words or phrases as you use in radio spots, or at least tie in with them very closely. This means, as far as you are concerned, you must know how many spots make an efficient buy on each of the stations you plan to use.

Assuming you already know all about which stations will reach your target audience best, you must now find out how many spots it will take to accomplish your specific purpose. Tell each rep how much you can spend, and ask him/her to recommend a schedule. In the meantime, sit down and figure out how you would do it. Comparing the two ideas, combining audience figures for specific dayparts with your available budget, will soon tell you how many spots to buy and where to place them. In most cases, you will do better to be sure you have enough spots on each station you actually use to gain a good frequency. It is better to do this than to spread your money and schedule very thinly over too many stations. If you have found that six to eight spots daily are required to do the job, then running three spots is probably a waste of money. If your budget won't stretch to running six to eight spots daily on three stations, drop back to the two best stations, being sure those two have enough spots to get you the necessary frequency.

For the same reason, be sure your spots on each station are run during the best times to reach your particular audience. If Station A reaches them from 6 to 10 a.m. and 3 to 7 p.m., and Station B does a better job from 10 to 3 p.m. and 7 to 10 p.m., then plan your buys accordingly. You may run some spots in all time periods on both stations, either for reasons of economy, or because you wish to reach each station's total audience for that day. But try to concentrate your heaviest schedule during the prime audience times.

This is the time to plan when each spot will run. To do this, you will need the rate cards, and some knowledge of how to read them. Some retailers and other small businesses tend to want to leave the actual placement of the spots up to the rep. This is fine, if you can trust the rep to do a good job. Initially, you will probably be better off to use the surveys and your own knowledge to do your own planning. As you find out whom you can trust, and begin to know which media work best, and what kinds of schedules bring you traffic, you can begin telling them how much you wish to spend, and letting them work out budgets to bring in for your approval. Until then, you may wish to make your own buys. This is one way of doing it:

OQQQ	Wed.	Thur.	Fri.		
6-10 AM	2	3	3	8 @ $_____	= $_____
10-3 PM	4	4	4	12 @ $_____	= $_____
3-7 PM	3	2	2	8 @ $_____	= $_____
					$300 Total

As you can see, if you plan each station this way, you will be able to place your spots where you want them, or where the available information tells you they will do the most good, and you will know exactly how much each spot will cost, how much each day will cost, and how much each station will cost over the length of the schedule. You will also know exactly what times during the day you can expect your spots to run on each station.

When you first start working out budgets, you will probably find that you haven't the slightest idea which money should go where. If you do, you may not know how many spots you will be able to buy for the money available. There are a couple of ways to begin working this problem out. First, decide how much money you will be spending in radio spots. Then divide it among the days you will be needing time. You may wish to give more money to the first two days of the schedule, and less to the last two, or equal weight to all days, or more to the first day, a little less to each successive day. You then divide the daily budgets among the stations, using the available audiences as the criteria.

Another way to plan is to allow each station so much of the budget for the sale, then divide that budget per station into days. Eventually, you will begin to know that a budget of $200, for instance, for a schedule on Station A might just as well not be spent, since it will buy you only six spots over a three-day period. Alternatively, you might find that you will need $500 to do the job.

You may have run two or three special events before you have any accurate reading on what station or newspaper ad can be expected to produce for you. It's a good idea to try and keep track of actual results, if you can. A newspaper ad can always carry a coupon. A spot on radio can tell listeners that a special discount will be allowed on an item if the person will tell his/her salesperson the magic word. If you make the word a different one on each station, and write each of them on a sheet of paper for the sales staff to mark, you will begin to have some idea of where your traffic is originating. Do make it very easy for the staff to mark the words. With several customers clamoring for attention, they will not have the time to write long reports, but they may have time to make a mark. Make a list of the stations down the left edge of the paper, leaving five or six spaces between them. In the next column, put the word for that station. Then draw lines between the stations, so there won't be any problem defining whose mark is whose. You should have a sheet that looks something like this:

Station A - "Snail"

Station B - "Wave"

Station C - "Work"

When a customer says the magic word, it entitles him/her to a special discount. All the salesperson has to do is make a mark in the right section. Later, you can tally the results and see which station brought you the most traffic. Of course, this isn't foolproof, since many people will not use the words. But if you do this type of thing two or three times, and two of the stations consistently outpull the third, you may want to weigh your media buys to take advantage of this.

After any special event, you may want to take a few minutes to analyze your results. This analysis may range from checking the gross sales figure, to assessing the damage done by all the three-year-olds, to finding out from all your staff what went wrong and right. Ask for suggestions to improve the whole thing. See if you can get an accurate traffic count for each day of the sale, as well as dollar figures for sales.

It is important to know how many people came in in response to the ads, since that is basically all the ads can accomplish. Even if you are selling a number of items for small prices, and you expect every person who walks in the door to buy two or three of them, the ad still has to bring them through the door. Once a person is looking at the sale items, he/she may well buy more than the one which attracted attention in your ad. The customer may also pick up that one item and leave. But whichever action the customer takes, unless you are running an ad for mail orders, the ad isn't going to make the cusotmer buy. This is most particularly true of any item which would rank in the customer's mind as a major purchase of any sort. Advertising pre-sells to some degree, but really gets the person to come to a place where he/she can see and touch and decide. So count your traffic.

Also, be aware of the fact that you probably will not be able to duplicate this sale the next time you try. If you run a very successful sale on September 10, 11, 12, and spend $2500 to do it, and attract 2,000 people a day, you will not duplicate these numbers the following month. This is even if your radio and television and newspaper ads are exact duplicates. The weather may be different, the economy will be different, the newspaper will place your ad in a slightly different position, the target audience you are trying to reach will have spent all its money getting the kids outfitted for school, or whatever. All you can do is try some different schedules and ideas, and see which ones work best. Then run them.

Try to think each campaign through carefully, being sure to give it the best you have. Produce quality ads to run in the best times and spaces you can afford. Hope for the best. If you are careful and spend wisely, you should get the results you are looking for, particularly if such special event campaigns have been supported previously by your annual advertising planning.

The Annual Budget

The first thing to do in planning your annual advertising is to look at and clearly define your goals. Start at ground zero, and move forward.

First, define and list your problems. Be concise and honest with yourself. Whether you are just beginning, or have been in business for a while and are looking for new directions, you need to define the problems. Do this before you can seek the solutions which will lead to your goals.

For instance, if you are a new company entering a field which has been dominated by an older firm offering the same products or services, your first problem might be to establish your name and obtain your share of the market. This means obtaining your share of the mind of your target audience. You need to decide what you want your share to be, and how fast you wish to move to obtain it. This will affect your budget and scheduling. To do this, you may have to do some research, or have a research firm do it for you. You need to know exactly how many people think first of that older firm, why they think of it, what they remember about it, and then how often they actually shop there, or whether they look there first/check out any smaller firms second/ decide where to make the purchase last.

Once you know this, and have carefully defined the target audience, you can begin planning a strategy which speaks directly to that audience. Even if you can spend only half of what the older firm spends on advertising, you can make a big dent in the field if your ads and spots are carefully designed and placed. A big dent can also be made if you take the time and trouble to refine whenever you can, and then bring in every bit of clear thinking you can toward building your public relations along with your advertising.

Beating the Competition

You may have to be very clever with your scheduling. One way to do this is to start your ads or spots one or two days ahead of the big blast by your competition. This gets the attention of potential customers before the competition does. You may wish to schedule your advertising very carefully to make it seem that you are doing as much or more than the competition.

Whatever your problems and goals, they need to be defined before you can begin planning. If your sales figures are too low, and your problem is the need to increase them, decide how much business is needed to give you the dollar figures you now have. Then figure out how much more traffic you need to accomplish the necessary increase. Then plan how to reach enough people with your advertising to bring in the traffic.

With each problem, decide on the solutions, and plan toward specific goals. If you do this, your advertising will build toward your goals, instead of putting out fires as they occur. No one can do this for you, and no book can tell you how to do it. You are the only one who knows your business well enough to seek out and define the problems, and then to figure out the solutions.

Once you have finished this part, you will be able to find help on the concrete parts of planning a specific ad (your artist), on buying a radio schedule (media reps), on writing a television commercial (your rep plus production staff).

After your problems and goals have been defined and listed, you are ready to begin planning. First, see what your seasons are, if you have them. Draw yourself a graph. Here's an example of one:

Figure 42. Graph for Determining Advertising Seasons.

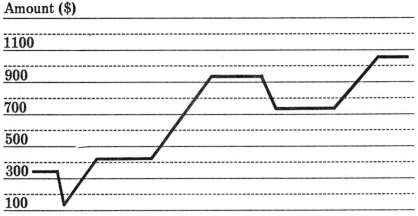

Amount ($)

1100

900

700

500

300

100

Jan. Feb. Mar. Apr. May Jun. Jul. Aug. Sep. Oct. Nov. Dec.

You can use ʝ ur actual fiscal year, or the calendar year, whichever suits you best. If you have already been in business for a year or two, use the chart like the above for planning your heavy and light advertising months. If you are just starting out in business, try using percentages of business (or simply figures from one to ten). The figure "1" would indicate a light month, and "10" is the heaviest month you expect within the coming year. Then plan your advertising schedules slightly in advance of the seasons, or heavy months. If you wish, plan them to beef up those months that are slow.

The Annual Budget Figure

To begin your actual budget plan, you may start with the annual budget figure. Then, divide that figure into monthly budgets. You may choose an even division, or you may choose to use more money some months than in others. For instance, if the total budget is $12,000, your budget might look like either of these two:

A $12,000		B $12,000	
January	$1000	January	$200
February	1000	February	300
March	1000	March	1200
April	1000	April	1300
May	1000	May	1500
June	1000	June	2500
July	1000	July	2000
August	1000	August	1500
September	1000	September	500
October	1000	October	500
November	1000	November	300
December	1000	December	200
	$12,000		**$12,000**

In the first case, you would have a steady kind of on-going ad plan which had the same weight every month, on the assumption that every month is of equal importance to your business and that seasonal buying makes no difference. In a case such as this, you might very well increase any of your monthly expeditures by use of co-op or trade-out ads which do not figure in your cash expenditures.

In case B, the advertiser has a very obvious and definite season, and advertising is planned around that season. Some advertising is placed each month, in order to keep the name and image of the company where the public will remain aware of it. But the bulk of advertising money is spent from March through August, with the other six months being less important. You need to decide how yours will work.

The Monthly Figure

Once you have decided how your budget will be spent on an annual basis, you must then begin to plan the actual media and expenditures for each month. Depending upon the kind of business in which you are engaged, you may want to get a calendar and go through it month-by-month at this point. Whichever type of plan you use, you will need to be aware of months in which big sales will fall, of holidays you may wish to use or to work around, of such things as vacation times for key employees which may affect the dates for the sales events. The object at this point is to decide when and how each month's money will be spent.

You may need to divide your budget into "Image" and "Product" advertising funds, as did the real estate firm used as an example in Chapter 4. The image ads may have to come solely out of your pocket, the product ads may be assisted with co-op funds. No matter whether your budget is divided or not, you will now need to begin deciding on specific media for specific dates. Look at the two examples in Chapter 4, then start your own month-by-month plan. Of course you may change it from time to time, but you still need a map of where you're planning on going. Media reps can be very persuasive, and without a plan like this one, even the most sales-resistant of us can sometimes get sidetracked.

When you are just beginning, it may help you to visualize the entire year. Try finding a cork board and a calendar with separate sheets. Tear the calendar apart, and pin the sheets side-by-side on the board. Each day should have a small square, so your cork board will look something like this:

Figure 43. Example of a calendar planning board.

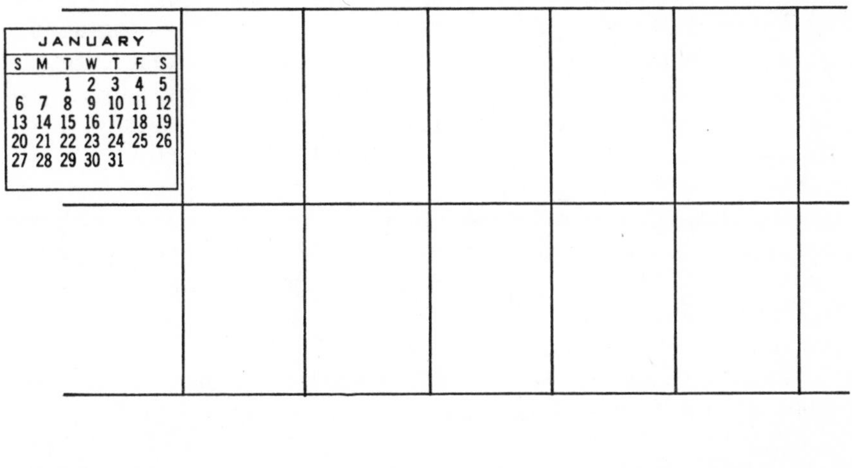

JANUARY					
S M T W T F S					

Once you have set it up, use a red pencil which can be erased, and mark in the important holidays you will use as special events. Note where your big selling seasons are, if you have them. Starting three to four weeks in advance of these seasons, pencil in ideas for newspaper and radio budgets, perhaps one week at a time. You might use a system of light diagonal lines in the days which will be heavy, so that you may later see them at a glance. Some people find that actually seeing their advertising planned out this way is a big help. For others, a simple one-page-per-month budget works just as well. In any case, use whatever method is easiest for you.

Once you have planned the basic money expenditures, you can start on the production end. In the budget examples we have just seen, no mention was made of production charges. They are very much a part of your advertising planning. It does you no good at all to have the best radio time in town, if your commercial is so badly produced that no one can understand either the name of your store nor what you're selling. So, right in this initial stage, plan what money will be available for use for each separate sale you have planned, for any ads running all year, or whatever. The production certainly shouldn't cost what the time or space will, but allow enough to get good quality ads for your money. To do this, you may draw on past experience or you may query your local newspaper, radio and TV stations for average costs to produce ads. At this stage your figures may be purely guesswork, and you may have to update and revise them as you actually begin to work on producing ads and commercials, but don't leave out the production charges entirely. At worst, you may have to indicate a very low figure which allows you to have one photograph made, or pays one person one time for a talent fee for radio. At best, you will allow enough money to do a bang-up job.

Your own budget and planning are the deciding factors, of course. You can sometimes run radio and newspaper ads for virtually no production charges, but television will normally cost you something, as will mechanical art necessary for magazines and other print media. Newspapers can usually set your ads for you at very little cost. Radio spots (when written by you) can be sent as scripts to each station, which will then produce its own spot to be aired in the schedule you bought on that station. They may run it "live" if you request, or they may record it. But your spot will not sound on one station exactly as it does on all the others.

This may or may not be an advantage. If your budget is limited though, you may not have a choice. Production money might allow you to use one person, with specific music or sound effects, to create the audio image which will do the best job for you. You can then have dubs made for every station you will use, so that your spot is the same on all stations. If this kind of thing is very important to your planning, you may have to see if you can chop some time off the schedule and use that money to produce your spots.

The important thing in this initial phase of your planning is to keep firmly in mind both time and space costs, and the expenses you will meet in order to fill the time and space with the best possible commercials or advertisements.

To help you do your budget, here's a step-by-step way to work out where and when the money should be spent. This budget is for a retail store which will have definite seasons when traffic is heavy, and other times when it is light. The owner has decided to build up the light times if possible by having some extra promotional events. The total budget for the year is $15,000.

From experience, the owner knows he will need some production money for the TV spot running prior to Christmas. He also knows he will need some funds for radio production, and a bit for new art for the newspaper and magazine ads. Before working out media buys, he allows a maximum production budget of $2,000, divided like this:

Total Budget For Production: $2,000

TV Spot—30 sec./Christmas Promotion............................$1,000
Radio spots—5 60-sec. spots for
                various promotions 500
Magazine ad—Pre-Christmas full-page
                in City Magazine/Dec............................... 100
Newspaper ads—Special Event ads with
                art and type charges 300

                                          1,900

Fund for extra expenses: $100

Even though the production budget is not large or complex, he has taken the time to lay it out in black and white, so he will know how much is available to spend for any particular project. He will know, in September or October, when he plans and produces his TV spot, that he cannot afford the suggestion by the station's production manager that they do an interview with Santa at the North Pole on location. Not that it might not be a good idea. But a good idea that costs more than the entire advertising budget is not a good idea for this advertiser, and he knows it. So, when he begins planning his annual TV spot, he will say to the production manager, "I can afford this much. Please work within that figure" and the production manager will do so.

There are inexpensive ways to make excellent television commercials. You may have to insist that you get a little attention from the production staff, and a little concentration on the problems, but if you are assertive without being aggressive, you should be able to get a decent spot for your money. Since TV costs range from low to very high indeed, there is no way to give you an accurate guess as to how much money you should put aside for television production in your city. The only thing you can do is go directly to those people who produce spots in your city and get estimates for spots. This means a low estimate and a high estimate. You may find that TV production is well within your budget, or you may find that you had best wait until you have a larger ad budget before trying television.

The retailer we are discussing (with his ad budget of $15,000) has just used $2,000 for production, leaving $13,000 for media. He now figures out a month-by-month plan for using this media money to best advantage. He knows his competition in town fairly well, and unless they change drastically for some reason, he can predict when they will do their heaviest advertising. They tend to have sales for holidays, and an occasional "seasonal" promotion of one sort or another. Their ad planning would look something like this:

January/February

White sale, as usual, entire month of January.

George Washington's Birthday Sale and Valentine's Day Sale in February.

March/April

Easter Sale, concentration on clothing.

May/June

Pool/Patio Furniture Sale, late May through early June.

Memorial Day special sale on Lawn Care items.

July/August

Very little advertising activity.

September/October

Back-to-School/Labor Day Sale—usually one week long.

Begin very small ad schedule in paper, leading up to Christmas.

These ads usually have specials on toys, to be put on lay-away.

November/December

Early November through Thanksgiving—concentration on two areas: First, the toy ads; Second, Home Furnishings and Decoration of the home for the holidays.

After Thansgiving, build from week-to-week in a steady schedule which peaks ten days before Christmas, then drops off very sharply, to virtually end three or four days before the 25th.

Our canny retailer, having watched this for two or three years, has made up his mind to work around this schedule. For instance, instead of having his White Sale in January, when people are a little short of cash due to Christmas spending, he decides to have it in March, and tie it in with re-decorating the house for spring. If he makes it a store-wide sale, and keeps his newspaper ads and radio spots running fairly consistently, he can add spots prior to Easter about outfitting the whole family at the same time you are decorating your home.

He may also have a sale in February, but it may be different from the usual holiday-based sale. He could have an "Early Bird Summer Sale," using left-overs from last summer, as well as some new items. He will try to have his advertising be slightly in advance of or different from his competitor's for the rest of the year, so his budget plan may look like this:

January/February

Small sale, mid-January, on Beauty Products to "Chase Away Those Winter Blues."

February

Lawn furniture sale, to make room for new stock, with drawing for above-ground pool, tied to advance swimsuit fashions. These two months, spend $1,500.

March/April

"Brighten Up the House for Spring" sale. White Sale combined with clothing for the family. Run mid-March through April. Toys for Easter tie-in. Spend $2,500

May/June

Spend $500, use radio one week out of each month for image only.

July/August

"Get Rid of Summer Blahs" Sale. "Shop Under the Stars"—a room decorated in dark blues and lights, with touches of white, and begin pushing specials for Christmas giving. Don't make it trite—all in excellent taste, with very nice items displayed for gifts, perhaps card-oriented service, some of the nicer, more expensive toys ready for lay-away. Spend $2,500.

September/October

Light advertising through about mid-October. Spend $1,000.

Mid-October—begin building Christmas traffic. Run donut radio and TV spots with lay-away products.

November/December

From beginning of ads in October through December 5th, spend perhaps $3,500. This is basically the place to run a week heavy, stay off several days, then come in heavy again. The last four to five days before Christmas, spend the remaining $1,500 in an effort to get all the last-minute traffic possible, since competition usually stops his ads no later than December 15th (or almost). A big push after that should attract attention.

This budget is rather casually worked, but it should give you some idea about how to do your own. It's wise to write down your reasoning, even if it is only a brief phrase or two, since three months from the time you decide on the budget, you may have no idea in the world why you thought you needed a full-page ad on March 17th.

You may wish to work out your own budget on the month-by-month basis we have just discussed, designating the media buy amounts for ongoing advertising as well as budgets for special events. Or, you may wish to look at it another way, depending on your area of business.

For instance, let us suppose you sell only one item, but it is a big, expensive one that most people will think about for some time before deciding to buy. They will probably only buy this item once in a lifetime, or only once every ten years or so. Your market/target audience is a very specialized one, and the age group/income factors are very definite. In this case, if you are just starting, you may have to budget from month-to-month, until you find out which media will do your job for you . Your planning may have to take the form of experimenting until you know which media reaches that audience and brings you results. Therefore, your budget might start out like this:

MONTH ONE:	Newspaper ads. Daily small ad, business page, large ads on Saturday and Sunday. $2,000
MONTH TWO:	Radio Station A—3 spots per day, drive times, two spots on Saturday morning. $2,000
MONTH THREE:	Combination of newspaper and Radio Station A. Spend $2,000 total, equally divided, planned to run opposite weeks during month with overlap on weekends.

At the end of this three-month period, an evaluation would be made to see which type of advertising did the best job. If none of it worked, the advertiser would have to consider something else, perhaps a direct mail campaign, magazine ads, or billboards. As you can see, this type of planning is different from the annual budget plan we have discussed so far. It is not an unusual way to plan, but the key here is that the advertiser *has planned*, and is checking results in order to know how to plan his/her entire year at some later point. The advertiser is not buying in an arbitrary manner. There are definite goals to reach, and different methods or paths are being used to reach those goals. When the advertiser finds the best way, planning is based on that method.

When you first start planning your annual budget, carefully investigate the various media, just as this advertiser is doing. You may find that one medium is by far the best for you to use. You may discover (and this is far more common) that you will need a "media mix" of one sort or another. There is research available to tell you how your reach and frequency will increase or decrease when you use a combination of media. Look at the budget figure for a specific period of time. Let's say four weeks. Then check whether you should spend it all on one media, or mix them. Some examples of media mixes are:

- ⅓ Newspaper + ⅔ Radio
- ⅓ Radio + ⅔ Television
- ⅔ Television + ⅓ Radio
- ⅓ Newspaper + ⅓ Radio + ⅓ Television

Talk with the reps in the various media in your town, and get hold of the research to glance through. You may be quite surprised to discover that putting all your eggs in one basket is not necessarily the best thing to do. Your budget will of course affect whether or not you can use two or more media. But, generally speaking, if you have any money available for advertising, you will spend it in more than one way. Don't say you cannot afford any specific media until you have quite thoroughly investigated the costs for space and time and production for all the media available in your city. You may find that at least your media mix will include newspapers, radio, and direct mail.

Below you will find a suggestion for topics to be included in your advertising plan for the year. If you use this as a base, along with a calendar and your ad budget, you should be able to plan your advertising at least a month in advance, even if you have just opened your business. If you are thinking of opening one, and are trying to decide on the financing you will need, you will do well to talk with your financial institution about funds for advertising. In drawing up an annual advertising plan, you will have a better idea of what to talk about if you are somewhat familiar with how such budgets are decided upon, and what sorts of decisions will need to be made concerning your advertising. This form is not for you to copy and use just as it appears. It is a sample to give you some basics for forming your own budget planning materials so that you may plan your own advertising just as an agency might do it for you.

You will probably want to make up your own form, using the topics and media which are of interest and use to you in your specific advertising planning. The thing you must keep in mind is that only through such planning will you be able to get the most value out of every dollar you spend on advertising.

Do the research to discover your target audience. Decide who you are, what you are selling, and to whom you are selling it. Become familiar with the media in your area, the costs for production. Decide what problems you have that must be overcome through your advertising, how you will go about this, and what specific goals you are trying to reach through advertising. Notice ads and commercials and special

Figure 44. Budget plan.

MONTH_____TOTAL BUDGET FOR MONTH:_____

WEEK BEGINNING:_____ENDING:_____WEEKLY BUDGET:_____

NEWSPAPER: AD DATES:_____;_____;_____;_____;_____

_____;_____;_____;

AD SUBJECTS/HEADLINES:_____;

_____;_____;_____;

PRODUCTION COSTS: BUDGET $_____. COMMENTS ON PROBABLE

PRODUCTION NEEDS, WITH ESTIMATES._____

_____

_____

RADIO: SCHEDULE DAYS AND STATIONS: MONDAY _____/_____/_____

BUDGET ALLOWANCE:$_____   _____/_____/_____
Station_____$_____
Station_____$_____   TUESDAY_____/_____/_____
Station_____$_____
Station_____$_____   _____/_____/_____

(And repeat for each of seven days for this week)

PRODUCTION ALLOWANCE: $_____COMMENTS ON PROBABLE SPOTS AND
PRODUCTION CHARGES, WITH ESTIMATES:_____

_____

TELEVISION TIME ALLOWANCE $_____PROBABLE DISTRIBUTION

AMONG STATIONS $_____$_____$_____$_____

PRODUCTION ALLOWANCE $_____FOR:_____

_____

OTHER MEDIA BUDGET:$_____(MEDIA)_____

$_____(MEDIA)_____

PRODUCTION ALLOWANCES: $_____FOR_____

$_____FOR_____

TOTAL BUDGET FOR MONTH: $_____TOTAL TIME/SPACE $_____

TOTAL PRODUCTION: $_____.

techniques. Do whatever reading in the field for which you have time. Keep in close touch with the media reps in your city. If you follow these guidelines, you should be able to spend your advertising dollars in such a way as to bring you the results needed to accomplish your goals.

Appendix

How to Select an Advertising Agency

Somebody once told me that selecting an ad agency is as complex as selecting a marriage partner. Certainly, in an ideal client/agency relationship, many of the factors are similar to those in a good marriage. Let's take a look at some of these factors, and then discuss the points you should look for when selecting your agency. As a client, there are several things you should be aware of as being your responsibility.

When you begin your search, try and find an agency which...

1....you like. This means more than liking the work they do for you and their other clients. You will be working very closely with these people, hopefully for an extended period of time. Try to find a group with whom you feel some degree of rapport; some liking. If you try to work with a person or group with whom you just don't feel comfortable, causing a personality conflict, you may find it difficult to believe what they tell you. Alternately, you might find it difficult to tell them what you really think and want.

2....you trust. Normally, in any close relationship, it takes some time to build total trust. This doesn't mean that when you select an agency you ought to blindly agree with every word they say. It *does* mean that before you hire them, you believe they can be trusted to do a good job, you believe they are honest with both money matters and opinions, and they indicate a strong belief in your company or products as being worthy of advertising.

3....you can communicate with. This means double-sided communication. If you have come up with what you think is the campaign idea to end them all, and you talk with the agency about it, be prepared for honest, open opinions. They may like it and think it will work. They may think it's the worst idea they've ever heard of. You need to allow them full freedom to say what they think. Be able to tell them what you think about something they have planned for you. The client/agency relationship has been compared to marriage, to the doctor/patient or lawyer/client relationship. The lines of communication must remain open, from you to them and from them to you, if the relationship is to work. As in any close working partnership requiring input from both partners, each needs the freedom to be honest without fear. Fear is an intangible part of a great number of client/agency relationships, and it doesn't make communication very easy. Certainly, if your agency comes up with an idea you dislike, you should say so. But don't hold over your agency the ever-present threat that you may fire them if they make a mistake. Tell them what the problems are, air things out openly, and ask them to fix whatever may be wrong. Then give them the chance to do it. This is a particularly wise idea if you have been dealing with them for some time, since they will expect it if the relationship is an open one. If you want your agency to do their best work for you, start out openly, and keep the lines open. The most certain way to freeze the agency and stop their creativity is to threaten to leave them.

    4.... has a good, solid reputation. We will get into detail about this aspect in a moment. For now, be aware that getting into the ad agency business has suddenly become almost as popular a sport as golf or tennis. Everybody's doing it. So before you start looking at specific agencies as possibilities, do a little research. Talk to your various media reps and see if you can find out which agencies have been in business long enough to gather some expertise, and long enough to establish their reputations. This is a good idea, mostly due to the fact that running a successful ad agency is more than placing media and sitting back counting all the commission money. It looks pretty good from the outside, but if you think about it, you will see that no agency can survive on the 15% commission alone. If the agency makes $150 from every $1,000 worth of advertising it places, they will have to place a lot of media buys to pay even the head of the agency and a secretary, not to mention the rent, lights, phone, and other bills. So try to find one that has been around long enough to be financially secure, as well as secure in their ability to create good advertising. These agencies are not hard to spot, but weed out the ones that don't meet your standards in this area.

    Before we discuss the ins and outs of judging agencies, let us look at what an agency does, and the people who perform the various functions. This will give you a clearer idea of the types of people with whom you may be working, even though you may never actually meet them.

Advertising agencies come in all sizes. There are "one-person" shops, and there are giants who employ hundreds of people in several branch offices throughout the United States and the world. No matter what the size, there are certain functions any full-service agency should be able to perform, whether one or two people run it, or one or two hundred are involved.

The first person you will deal with in any agency is the man or woman who functions as the "account executive." This may be the head of the agency (in a small shop) or one of several people who function solely as the liason between you (the account) and the agency personnel. In larger agencies, each account exec may handle only one large account. In smaller shops, each may handle several. In the one-person shop, obviously there is only one person who handles all the accounts. Whatever the size of the agency, the person you deal with should be enthusiastic about your business or products; should be willing to inform him/herself about any and all aspects of your business, its problems, its goals, its history. Account execs should know all they can about media. They should be able to communicate well with you, with your advertising manager (if you have one), and with their own co-workers. To be any good, they will have to know almost as much about your business as you do, for only in this way can they help define the problems, formulate the goals, and create the solutions.

In most agencies, once the account exec has signed you up as a new account, there will be certain matters which must be learned by the agency before they can come up with any suggestions. This involves research, either into your business or products to find the best points to advertise, or the problem areas to be confronted, or into such matters as your share of the market or mind of your target audience as it currently exists (or as you would like it to exist). Research might even delve into finding out if there is a customer target for whatever you are selling. During this period, you will be involved either directly or indirectly with the person(s) in charge of "marketing research." There may or may not be a separate department for this in a smaller shop, but any good agency will perform this function for every new client.

After the research has been performed, and a strategy approach solidified, the agency begins to perform two functions that are inter-related. One is planning and buying the media. The other is planning and creating the actual advertisements. Whether the two are handled by one person or twenty, the same things are involved. The media planning and buying is done almost the same way you did it for yourself. In most cases, the agency will go into far more detailed research as to which media will be best used to accomplish your goals, how much of each will be needed, and how they will be used in conjunction with one another to achieve the best possible results. While this planning is going on, the "Creative Services" department will be planning print and broadcast advertisements that tell your target audience exactly what they need to know about your product or service.

Other basic funcitons of many full-service agencies can include:

A Public Relations (PR) department to assist with getting your name or the name of your product into the eye of the public by other means than paid advertising.

An accounting department which carefully checks to be sure all your media has run as scheduled and if not, why not. They will also monitor whether or not you will receive makegoods. This department also checks all the bills from the media for accuracy and against the schedule as contracted. They send you your bill, and generally handle all financial transactions for the agency.

Large agencies may have one or more people performing the following functions, but for the most part, they will fall into one of the broad categories above. Such people may include artists, photographers, copywriters, casting directors, radio production chiefs, television production chiefs, designers, secretaries, clerks, copy boys or girls, or others. In any case, they all have one aim in a good agency: to provide you with the best advertising possible.

Once you have selected your agency, do keep in mind that it is not necessarily a good idea to be penny-wise and dollar-poor. Advertising agencies provide a needed service, but they are not by any means in business for the pure fun of it. If they are going to do a good job, they must have enough money to do it, and to make money themselves. Any agency who is losing money on an account will not give its best efforts to that account, and will eventually dump it. Some agencies work purely on the basis of 15% commission on media, plus the mark-up on any non-commissionable work, combined with whatever the hourly charge is for agency services. Other agencies work on the basis of a retainer, a fee you pay every month, plus actual cost of any art or service performed. Still others charge a small retainer, plus the commissions from media, plus costs for outside or internal services performed.

No matter which method your agency uses, expect it to make money for handling your account. If you are relatively small, you may have to work with a smaller agency, one that can afford to grow along with its clients. In any case, be sure that all monetary matters are perfectly clear before you start. Be sure the agency you propose to deal with is honest, that they understand your budget and aims, and that they feel free to come to you at any time with money problems so that you can decide what to do if a decision is called for.

If you want the best advertising possible, keep in mind that there are human and mechanical factors involved. Don't make the agency pay through the nose if they make a mistake. If you have authorized a television spot for which slides must be taken, you can reasonably expect them to make good on that quote. However, suppose for some reason the slides were fuzzy, not usable, or had to be re-taken. Don't dump the entire cost of the new session on the agency. You may not be able to absorb the cost yourself, but such an expense should be shared. Perhaps the photographer is not at fault and is willing to donate his time to make it good, but cannot absorb the cost of film and processing. You and the agency might share that expense.

This is not to say you should pay and re-pay for inadequacies or careless mistakes on the part of your agency. I do think that if you have confidence in the agency and the work they do, however, that you can expect an occasional mistake without flying off the handle. If the agency has blatantly ordered twelve dubs of the wrong spot, there is no reason for you to pay for them; the agency should. On the other hand, if the agency has done its job and something still goes wrong, at least talk it over before you expect them to absorb the entire cost. Doing this will allow your agency to know that you expect the best, and they will not be afraid to tell you if something is not up to par for some reason. In the long run, you will be the beneficiary.

There are good agencies, mediocre agencies, and downright bad agencies. There are, fortunately, ways to tell which is which. That should make you feel better. For the sake of convenience, we will discuss several "types" of agencies, some of which would be good for a small advertiser, and some which would be disastrous.

Throughout the following discussion, bear in mind the points we have already talked about. No matter which "type" of agency you are looking at, consider all the above points, as well as those we will look at now. Also keep in mind that we are looking at a business in one basic geographical area, with one (or perhaps as many as two or three) stores or outlets, being handled by agencies dealing solely on a local (or perhaps as much as a regional or statewide basis) and whose clients fall into the same type of category. For instance, an agency in your city may very well handle the state Tourism account. This would involve media buys both within and without the state. But probably no agency we are discussing here would handle the advertising for a national account involving media purchases in every state and some foreign countries, and dealing in millions of dollars on network TV or radio.

The Big Guys. To this type of agency, you will be a very small fish in a big pond full of bigger fish. In most cases, this type of agency won't handle small accounts unless they have recently lost one of the biggies and need to fill a gap until they can land another big one. At this point, if they hear of two or three accounts the size of yours, they may make an active effort to sign you up. They will tend to milk your budget for all they can, until some bigger account comes along, and then sort of drop you into a limbo of secretaries and new account execs. There may be little or no attention or service until you finally become disgusted and leave.

A good agency of this size will tell you at the beginning that you do not need them; you need a smaller house where you can receive just the right amount of attention until you have grown enough to need their services. However, the burden of the decision is on you. There are probably relatively few agencies of the type we are discussing who could resist the chance to sign you on. Look closely at any of the larger agencies in your city before signing up with them. You may find that they handle advertising for some of the largest businesses in the area, and therefore will not be interested enough to give your smaller account the attention it needs.

The Award Winners. In this corner, we have the agencies who work terrifically hard, with one major goal in mind. They are out to win awards. Unfortunately, that doesn't necessarily mean winning customers for their clients. The ads created by this type of agency will be slick, clever, beautiful, up-to-date, trendy, and out to attract attention.

But the attention will be attracted to the ad itself, and then to the agency. One way to spot this type of agency is through the advertising they produce. If the ads attract attention to themselves, but not to the product or business they are supposed to be selling, the agency is probably more concerned with building its own portfolio than with building your business. A good ad, of course, if entered in a contest, may win an award—but the ad should be designed to do a job for the *advertiser*, not specifically to win an award.

The Assembly Line. This agency can be any size at all. The one feature which makes it stand out is the fact that it does very little individualized work for its clients. The owner (or perhaps the owner and his creative director/partner) found a formula that worked for one client and decided that you should never fool with success. Every ad, spot, campaign, budget, or whatever, coming out of the agency since that one success has many similarities. Now, even if no new work is done, if the agency has been careful in building its client list, they will have managed to stay in business. If the formula that worked for a furniture store will work for an insurance company, and also for a dry cleaning shop and a restaurant, it's very possible the agency could be in business and making a living when you come along. So look carefully at samples of work the agency has produced, at campaign planning, and at how much research has gone into the plans for any new client, as well as how much they plan to do for you. If there is a great deal of similarity in planning an ad campaign for all the clients in one agency, you may wish to look around a little more.

The Presentationists. There are agencies who do a fantastic job of selling you on the fact that they are the very best. Their strength lies in figuring out how best to present themselves to prospective clients, and in making a lovely presentation which seems to be just-what-you-have-always-dreamed-of. However, always check an agency's client list, and if they seem to have gained and then lost a lot of clients, they may not have the expertise or the ability to do the plain hard work which must be done. They may be able to create a campaign which gets you off to a good start, but have no idea where to go from there. There is a big difference between getting clients and keeping clients. You need an agency with the skills to let you know in the beginning that they can do your specific job and then continue to perform in a way that will keep you with them. Find out, if you can, how long the clients on any agency's list have been with them. If you run across an agency who makes an impressive presentation and whose client list has remained stable, keep them in mind as a possibility.

The Small Guys. To this type of agency, your account may look like the moon on a silver platter. The agency may be one or two people, or even a few more. But most of their accounts are fairly small, and they handle a large number of them. This type of agency may not have enough expertise to do a good job for you. That is, if they have been used to placing (and creating) one or two small newspaper ads per month, and an occasional radio spot, and every now and then a magazine ad for twenty or thirty accounts, they may not have the knowledge and abilities needed to do your research. They may not be able to come up with marketing and creative planning ideas for a full campaign, and carry the project through to completion. Don't look at agencies which are too small in size and in thinking to handle your business. You may seem like a windfall to them, and they may try very hard to do the job, but the fact remains that there are a number of advertising agencies run by people who should be selling shoes.

The categories above are arbitrary selections. You may find an agency which combines several of these major types, or you may find others which have other problems that make them less than ideal. Whatever the problems, there ought to be some agencies who seem to have none of them, or at least very few. There are also positive points you can consider when you are looking for an agency.

First, try to find one which is sincerely interested in creating the kind of advertising any specific client needs. That means they will make every effort to discover what needs to be accomplished. They will then go to work to come up with exactly the right planning to do the job. Such an agency will be interested in your total business. If you are in doubt what color to choose for the carpet in your reception area, this agency will be glad to help.

The Total Picture

If you can find an agency that is sincerely concerned with helping your business grow, in providing you with any and all creative services you may need, in supporting you with PR suggestions, and doing everything possible to help your business move in the direction you want it to go, take a look at it. This type of agency, no matter what its size, is eager to keep you as a client. It is willing to help you grow, as it is growing with you, so that you build the kind of lasting relationship that will be a good thing for both of you. A good agency can be anything from one person to twenty or more, if each person at the agency is involved and eager to supply you with the advertising services you need. If you like them, and they like you and your products, and they would like to work with you, it is probably wise to consider them more closely.

Once you have reached this stage, there are some things you can check to be sure you are making a good decision. We have covered many of them in this section. Others may be obvious to any business person, while other factors may not be so familiar. There is really no way to guarantee that any agency you select (no matter how carefully) will be all that your research shows it to be. However, if you do no checking at all, if you simply call a bunch of agencies in and invite them to give a presentation, you may get burned. Even an agency with a well-known name and reputation should be checked before you sign with it.

Things change. In advertising, they may change from one week to the next. So don't go on reputation alone. If you can talk with some current clients, do so. Check with the Better Business Bureau and with the media to be sure the financial picture is stable. Once you have done this, you will then want to look at other work performed by the agency, as well as whatever presentation they have made for you.

Progress Checkpoints

It is sometimes difficult to tell you how to choose. One thing should be obvious, though. Any work performed for clients should be geared toward accomplishing specific advertising goals. It should be designed especially for each client, not merely changed in minor ways, so that ads for one client cannot be told from ads for another except for name changes. The agency should be large enough to do your job, but not so large that your relatively small account gets lost. They should be enthusiastic about your business or product, confident of their ability to handle your work, and should express an interest in working with you. Allow presentations from six agencies which you have culled from the group in your city to make presentations. After they have all visited you, and one of them writes a note saying, "Thank you for the opportunity. We would really like to work with you and believe we can do an excellent job," by all means consider them! If they care enough to do this sort thing, they may just care enough to do a good job for you. If their skills are what you need, and they are stable, you may wish to hire them.

Understand how and what they will charge. Start at Day One and build a lasting relationship which is open, honest, trusting, and trustworthy on both sides. You would not like it if your agency told other people that yours is a bad place to do business because you had one unhappy customer who called the agency and complained. By the same token, if the agency goofs, there is no need for you to spread it all over town. Both you and your agency should feel free to discuss any problems which may arise.

And by the way, if they do a good job, tell them so. Those open lines of communication should work for problems *and* for compliments.

A good agency/client relationship, when formed between a business and the right agency, can last many years and be of great benefit to both parties. When you are ready to select your agency, try to do it with that idea in mind. It is usually a mistake to try to get the slickest ads for the least money in the shortest time possible. Work with your agency to build the relationship. If the first time you try is not successful, remember, everyone makes mistakes. Don't let one mistake sour you on agencies. If you are ready to find one, somewhere you will find the right one for you.

Index